# PREHISTORIC
# PATHFINDERS
## PIONEERS OF ENGLISH ARCHAEOLOGY

*In memory of Thomas Bateman, whose
life and work
first aroused my interest
in matters archaeological.*

# PREHISTORIC PATHFINDERS

## PIONEERS OF ENGLISH ARCHAEOLOGY

BARRY M. MARSDEN

FONTHILL

Fonthill Media Limited
www.fonthillmedia.com
office@fonthillmedia.com

First published in the United Kingdom 2014

Copyright © Barry M. Marsden 2014

ISBN 978-1-78155-353-4

The right of Barry M. Marsden to be identified as the author of this
work has been asserted by him in accordance with the Copyright,
Designs and Patents Act 1988.

Typeset in 10pt to 13pt Sabon LT Std

Printed and bound by CPI Group (UK) Ltd, Croydon, CR0 4YY

# Introduction

This work draws together a series of pen-portraits of some 40 individuals who helped shape the foundations of English prehistoric study, mainly during the eighteenth and Nineteenth centuries. They were a diverse cross-section of society, and included army officers, reverends, country squires and gentry, bankrupts, suicides, a probable illegitimate royal, a high churchman, a tradesman and a farmer, plus a scion of the nobility and a superintendent of a 'lunatic asylum.' My list is of necessity subjective as I deemed it essential to have a portrait of each individual and some who might well have been included have been omitted for the apparent lack of any surviving image.

As well as portraits, short biographies of each personality are embellished with appropriate illustrations, including digs, artefacts, archaeological sites and some of their more interesting tombs, together with other images connected with their activities. The work will hopefully stand as an entertaining and instructive 'who's-who' of these early activists, whose lives have long fascinated me, together with an assessment of their importance in the study of the origins of English archaeology.

# Acknowledgements

In preparing this book I would like to thank the following for their help in providing images and information on the individuals whose lives are the subject of the work:

The Society of Antiquaries of London; the Ashmolean Museum, Oxford; Avebury Museum; Trustees of the British Museum; Buxton Museum and Art Gallery; Cheltenham Museum and Art Gallery; Creswell Heritage Trust; Devon Life; Dorset County Museum; Guernsey Museum and Art Gallery; Hull and East Riding Museum; Stephen Harrison; Adrian James; Liverpool Museums; Eric Miller; Maureen Morris; Radnor, Midsomer Norton and District Museum Society; Chris Smith; Scarborough Museum; Sheffield Archives; Sheffield City Museum; Wiltshire Heritage Museum.

Any omissions in acknowledgement relating to any image is unintentional and will be rectified in any future edition of this work.

# PORTRAITS OF PIONEERS

# AKERMAN, John Yonge (1806–1873).

John Yonge Akerman (1806-73),
archaeologist, numismatist, angler and
long-term official of the Society of
Antiquaries.

Akerman was born in London in June 1806, son of a merchant. At an early age he was appointed secretary to the radical politician and writer William Cobbett. Subsequently he became secretary to Lord Albert Conyngham (later Lord Londesborough). Elected FSA in 1834 he became joint secretary of the society in 1848, and sole secretary five years later. He also edited the society's journal *Archaeologia*, holding both posts until 1860 when he resigned through ill-health. Though interested in antiquities in general, his two specialities were digging (particularly barrows) and numismatics. He personally founded the first English journal to focus on coinage, the *Numismatic Journal*, in 1836, and helped establish the Numismatic Society of London that same year, acting as secretary until 1860 and editing its own periodical the *Numismatic Chronicle*. In 1849 he published the first ever distribution map of British coins.

As an active archaeologist Akerman dug extensively, firstly in Kent on Lord Albert Conyngham's estates in the early 1840s, then in Wiltshire, Berkshire and neighbouring areas; his investigations focused mainly on the prehistoric and Anglo-Saxon periods. His plans and sections of certain tumuli show some insights into the information such pursuits could provide, though his

*Interior of the Eastern half of the Barrow, shewing the situation of the Urns, and the extent of the excavation.*

Akerman's unusual method of illustrating a series of Bronze Age urn burials found in a Wiltshire barrow.

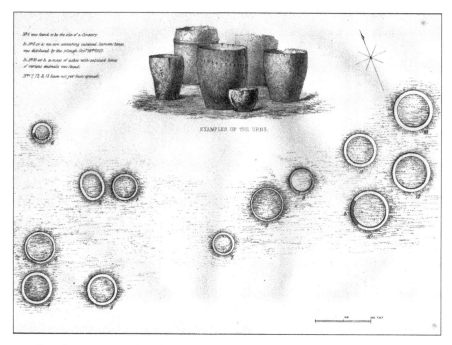

EXAMPLES OF THE URNS.

Excellent for its time is this plan of Bronze Age ring ditches explored at Standlake in Oxfordshire in 1857 with illustrations of the urns found at the site.

wry pessimism showed through in his comments on digging on the Wessex downland. 'Experience' he wrote 'has taught me not to anticipate great things from excavations. I had learned long ago, that a rude and crumbling urn, or a simple heap of ashes and calcined bones, were the frequent result of a whole day's digging in these early sepulchral mounds.' He commented elsewhere of 'tedious, irksome and laborious' operations, but was 'persuaded that such excavations were not altogether profitless'!

His more important operations included work on a series of ring barrows at Standlake in Oxfordshire in 1857 with Stephen Stone, proving the prehistoric antiquity of the monuments, and the investigation of two Anglo-Saxon cemeteries at Brighthampton and Long Wittenham in Berkshire, in 1857 and 1859. His written works included two archaeological contributions, an *Archaeological Index for Celtic, Romano-British and Anglo-Saxon Remains* (1847) and *Remains of Pagan Saxondom, Principally from Tumuli in England* (1855). Akerman was alert to the increasing plundering of barrows in his time, noting that 'no inconsiderable number' had been destroyed 'under the hands of pseudo-antiquaries.'

A keen angler, Akerman's other interests included provincial dialect words, tradesmens' tokens and legends. In recognition of his contributions in several spheres, especially his published works on Roman coins relating to Britain, he was awarded the gold medal of the French Institute, and was made an honorary member of several learned societies. He died at his home in Abingdon in November 1873.

# ATKINSON, John Christopher (1814–1900).

John Christopher Atkinson (1814–1900), 't'auld Canon' who served the parish of Danby in North Yorkshire for over 40 years, and opened between 80-100 prehistoric cairns in the vicinity of his home.

Described as 'a man of great mental and physical energy, and of multifarious interests' Atkinson was born in May 1814 at Goldhanger in Essex, son of a curate. He graduated from Cambridge in 1838 and after curacies in Hereford and Scarborough, gained the living of Danby in the North Riding of Yorkshire in 1847 as the gift of Viscount Downe. Atkinson married three times and fathered thirteen children, some of whom proved useful workers on his antiquarian expeditions.

'T'auld Canon's' earliest study was ornithology; he published several books on the subject, and when at Danby, on the remote moors of the district, he became absorbed in the customs, place-names, dialect and folklore of the locality. Histories of Cleveland and Whitby were the fruits of these studies, whilst he also edited a series of local medieval and later documents, including the Rievaulx Chartularies. An undoubted success was his entry into the realms of schoolboy fiction, with his popular tales of juvenile expeditions.

As an antiquary Atkinson explored some 80–100 prehistoric cairns in the vicinity of his Danby vicarage, most of them within a five-mile radius of his home. Described by Canon Greenwell as 'a diligent and careful digger' he also assisted the Canon in his extensive operations, persuading him to publish his voluminous *British Barrows* (1877), of which he made a fair copy of more

Atkinson and his third wife, Helen, pose in the garden of Danby Rectory sometime in the late 1880s. The lady in question was some fifty years his junior!

Typical of the many cairns Atkinson explored on the North York moors is Flat Howe, which still retains its surrounding kerb.

than half. Atkinson recorded, in a series of scattered reports, his openings of Cleveland burial mounds, but Frank Elgee in his *Early Man in North-East Yorkshire* (1930) could only trace details of some 33. His collection comprised 43 urns of varied types, plus jet beads, stone axes and flint tools and weapons. They were presented to the British Museum, but the Canon's inadequate labelling has left many unprovenanced. He was also less than precise about the location of the many cairns he excoriated, and regrettably he failed to draw his results together in book form, or publish any plans, sections or maps of the barrow groups he dug.

By all accounts Atkinson was a man of cantankerous disposition, clashing with the printer and patron of his Cleveland history, and expressing his displeasure when the Wolds barrow-digger John Mortimer trespassed on his territory by operating on Easington Moor. He also complained to Thomas Bateman that the latter's proxy digger, James Ruddock, was encroaching on his preserves by opening barrows on the local moors. Atkinson died in March 1900 at the vicarage where he had spent over 50 years ministering to his flock. Perhaps his most enduring record was his *Forty Years in a Moorland Parish* (1891), a mine of historical and antiquarian knowledge, and a classic account of a rural ministry in Victorian England.

# AUBREY, John (1626–1697).

John Aubrey (1626–1697), scholar, writer and antiquary, once described as 'mad as anyone almost in the university of Bedlam.'

Described by a contemporary as 'mad as anyone almost in the university of Bedlam', John Aubrey was born in March 1626 at Easton Pierse in Wiltshire, eldest son of a landowner with estates in Wiltshire and Herefordshire. He was educated at Oxford, and his father's death in 1652 gained him property, but also his parent's considerable debts. His prospects for relief were hampered, first by the death of a prospective rich heiress as a wife, and his later acquaintance 'in an ill howre' with an unsuitable lady who he almost married; subsequent legal proceedings exhausted his assets, as he had been forced to sell his Hereford properties some years earlier. By 1671 his impecuniousness forced him into a life of a peripatetic scholar, dependent on friends and patrons for board and hospitality. The rest of his life was one of constant near poverty and dependence.

The range of Aubrey's intellectual interests and his contribution to many fields of study, which included architecture, folklore, mathematics, and biographical works, are matters for a wider study, as here we concerned with his antiquarian pursuits. The ancient landscape of Wiltshire helped nurture his interest in the subject, stimulated by his discovery of the Avebury megalithic monument in 1649. He attended Charles II on his visit to the West Country in 1663, and surveyed Avebury at the monarch's request. He later examined Stonehenge, discovering the ring of pits inside the encircling ditch that now bear his name, picked out by the rays of the setting sun late one summer evening.

By 1693 Aubrey had completed the manuscript of his great work *Monumenta Britannica,* the foundation text of British archaeology, describing 'druid temples', Roman towns, castles, camps, barrows and other sepulchral monuments, together with urns, coins, roads, ditches and camps. Many of the sites he described have since disappeared or have been significantly altered. Regrettably this major antiquarian work languished in manuscript in the Bodleian Library until its publication some 280 years after its author's death! Of his activities he wrote 'My head was alwaies working; never idle and even travelling (which from 1649 till 1670 was never off my horseback) did gleane som observations . . . . some whereof are to be valued.' His accounts of prehistoric field monuments remain for the most part objective and free from the fancies and wild speculations of his successors, though he did bequeath the ubiquitous Druids as a legacy, later gleefully approved by William Stukeley and others, which plagued prehistoric archaeology for long enough!

Aubrey's fund of stories and quick wit must have made him amusing company, a convivial and eccentric gossip, whom many thought 'a little crazed.' He died in May 1697 and was buried in Oxford. Only in the latter part of the last century was the significance of his contribution to many branches of scholarship really appreciated. He can fairly be said to have laid the groundwork for establishing the principles of field archaeology. He was a pathfinder, in many ways in advance of his time, acute in perception, exuding buoyant cheerfulness with an entertaining and whimsical manner.

# BAGSHAWE, Benjamin (1845–1907).

Benjamin Bagshawe (1845–1907), solicitor and antiquary, who dug the most prolific prehistoric barrow in Derbyshire between 1866 and 1868.

Born in Eyam, Derbyshire in 1845, Bagshawe, described by a contemporary as 'a gentleman well-versed in local lore and an antiquarian and local archaeologist' practised as a solicitor in Sheffield. He was also a genealogist and historian and a member of the Sheffield Literary and Philosophical Society. He excavated the Long Low round cairn on his property at Grindlow in 1861, finding a beaker and several skeletons and publishing the results in the quarterly magazine the *Reliquary,* edited by Llewellynn Jewitt.

Between 1866–1868 Bagshawe organised a dig on another round cairn at Hazlebadge, near Bradwell in the Derbyshire Peak. The burial mound was one of the most prolific ever opened in the county, producing a wealth of early Bronze Age inhumations and cremations, several of the former in stone cists, together with beaker, food-vessel and urn pottery, and bronze, jet and stone artefacts. Sadly the dig was never properly published, apart from a few notes and rough plans. Few of the finds have survived, and these consist of two beakers and a food-vessel, all in Sheffield City Museum. The food-vessel was presented to the museum before 1893, but the beakers only surfaced, together with the scrappy notes and plans, in 1956 when the vast and badly-preserved Bagshawe family collection was presented to the Sheffield Museum archive. There are no records of any further barrow openings by Bagshawe before his death in 1907.

The Hazlebadge round cairn sits on an eminence above Bradwell in the Peak District. Sadly its excoriation was not accomplished with any great expertise, even by the standards of the 1860s.

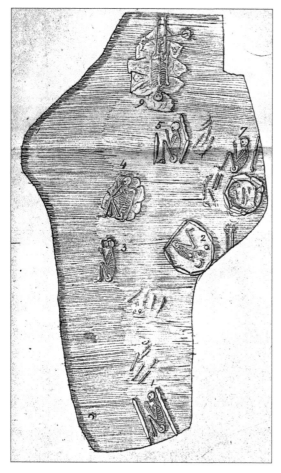

Bagshawe's rough sketch plan of 1866 reveals a variety of burials of high interest though most of the finds have long since disappeared.

# BATEMAN, Thomas (1821–1861).

Thomas Bateman (1821–61), Derbyshire country squire, archaeologist and collector who dug some 200 burial mounds in his native county during his short life, preserving the relics and publishing his researches in two books.

Born at Rowsley, Derbyshire, in October 1821, Thomas Bateman can be regarded as one of the Nineteenth century's archaeological pioneers. He was the son of a country gentleman and the grandson of a cotton merchant who retired to his native county and bought an estate at Middleton-by-Youlgrave. Thomas's mother died whilst he was an infant and his father when he was thirteen, and he was brought up by his grandparent at Middleton. At his coming of age Thomas inherited his father's wealth and fled the clutches of his grandfather; he fell in with a young married woman and took her to live with him at his newly built mansion, Lomberdale House, just outside Middleton. He was an early member of the British Archaeological Association (BAA) where he met fellow like-minded antiquaries who remained lifelong friends.

Bateman's father had dug a few of the local tumuli, and Thomas, perhaps inspired by the folios of Richard Colt Hoare's *Ancient History of Wiltshire*, embarked, from 1843, on a campaign of barrow-digging, mainly in the Derbyshire and Staffordshire Peak which resulted in the excoriation of over 200 burial mounds, plus a further 200 opened by his Stafford and Yorkshire proxies, Samuel Carrington and James Ruddock. His mansion embodied a purpose-built museum which not only housed his barrow collections, but an eclectic and growing assemblage of other material.

In 1847 Bateman's grandfather died, and prompted by the provisions of his will, Bateman jettisoned his mistress and speedily married the sister of his barrow-digging companion, William Parker. The union produced five

A sketch of Bateman's dig at Taylor's Low, Wetton in 1845 shows him wielding a pick on top of the mound. Most of the other workers can be identified from Isaacson's poem *Barrow-Digging by a Barrow Knight*.

Operations at Gib Hill near Youlgrave in 1848 reveal a dangerous undercutting into the south side of the huge cairn, which may have originated as a Neolithic mound, later enlarged in the Early Bronze Age.

*Above left:* Bateman's tomb, sited in a field behind the old chapel at Middleton-by-Youlgrave, is surmounted by a stone replica of a Bronze Age urn.

*Above right:* William Parker (1816–94), Bateman's barrow-digging friend and later brother-in-law, here depicted in Isaacson's poem as a 'Distinguished Barrow Opener.'

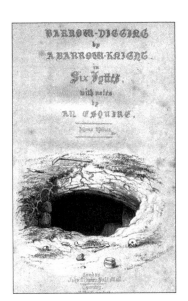

*Above left:* The frontispiece to Isaacson's work depicts the opening of a cist on Harthill Moor, Derbyshire. The burials were by cremation, hence the skull and bones appear by courtesy of artistic licence!

*Above right:* The Revd Stephen Isaacson (1798–1849), author of the poem on a typical Bateman expedition, has been described as 'by no means an ornament to the church.'

daughters and a son, Thomas junior. Usually referred to thereafter as 'the Squire' Bateman was a reserved and outwardly distant personality whose character was nicely exemplified by Elizabeth Meteyard in her 1870 children's novel, *Dora and her Papa,* a work based on Bateman himself. In 1848 he published his first book, *Vestiges of the Antiquities of Derbyshire,* a digest of all local barrow-digging from 1759, plus details of his own delvings.

Bateman was an archaeological pathfinder in many respects. He drew plans and sections of the tumuli he dug, and preserved not only human bones, but those of other creatures found in the mounds, plus pottery and other artefacts, including scraps of material other diggers routinely ignored. He noted the skull forms of individuals, remarking on the differences between those found in the large chambered cairns of the Peak, and others exhumed from the later, smaller, round barrows. The term 'long barrow, long skull, round barrow, round skull' might well have originated with him. As time passed Bateman's archaeological appetite waned, perhaps as a result of his growing interest in other branches of collecting (he published a catalogue of his museum in 1855), the pressures of running his burgeoning estates, and the growing scarcity of sites to dig.

In 1861 Bateman produced his second barrow book, *Ten Years' Diggings in Celtic and Saxon Grave-Hills in the Counties of Derby, Stafford and York,* a continuation not only of his own Derbyshire excavations, but those of his proxies in Stafford and Yorkshire. He died in August 1861 at the early age of 39, and was buried on a hillside at Middleton in a railed tomb surmounted by a stone representation of an Early Bronze Age collared urn.

Though Bateman's operations are not without criticism, they were exemplary for their time; every tumulus he dug was written up and published, many were drawn in plan and section, and even the smallest finds were preserved. The extensive barrow-openers of the later Nineteenth century all paid due homage to him and his archaeological collection remains intact, though not in its native Derbyshire where it should reside, but in Sheffield City Museum, where, since the institute's revamping in 2007 it is largely confined to storage. Sadly, the rest of Bateman's extensive museum collection was sold off to pay the bills of his improvident son.

Mention should be made here of Bateman's friend, bailiff and later brother-in-law, William Parker (1817–1894), a constant companion who was invariably present at the Squire's digs. Another strong personality associated with Bateman was the Revd Stephen Isaacson (1798–1849) whom the Squire met at the first BAA gathering at Canterbury in 1844. Described as 'by no means an ornament to the church' the cleric took part in Bateman's 1845 barrow campaign, and later wrote the amusing, witty and instructive little poem *Barrow-Digging by a Barrow-Knight,* based on that summer's activities. Sadly the pair fell out, largely due to Isaacson's duplicity, and the work was never properly publicised.

# BORLASE, William Copeland (1848–1899).

William Copeland Borlase (1848–99) Cornish gentleman, MP and archaeologist, whose career was ruined by scandal and bankruptcy.

Born near Penzance, Cornwall, into a wealthy family in 1848, Borlase was the great grandson of the Revd William Borlase (1696–1772), antiquary and naturalist who had published his *Antiquities of the County of Cornwall* in 1754. Borlase senior dug several barrows in his native Cornwall in the 1750s, and had also visited the Isles of Scilly where he examined some of the Scillonian entrance graves, producing careful plans of those he cleared.

William Copeland Borlase was doubtless influenced by the work of his great grandfather, and from an early age visited many of the ancient monuments in the county. Whilst still in his 'teens he helped supervise work at the prehistoric settlement and fogou at Carn Euny, of which he produced an account in 1864. Educated at Oxford, he was called to the bar at Inner Temple, and also served as a JP and a Deputy Warden of the Stanneries of Cornwall and Devon. He was also elected FSA for his work on the primeval antiquities of his locality.

Borlase was certainly opening Cornish tumuli by the later 1860s, subsequently commenting that he had dug 'upwards of two hundred sepulchral mounds' though leaving details of only twenty-two. His *Naenia Cornubiae* of 1872 was not only a record of some of his excavations but information on other barrow explorations in the county, with eccentric observations on the origin and purpose of the megalithic monuments of the area. He wrote a

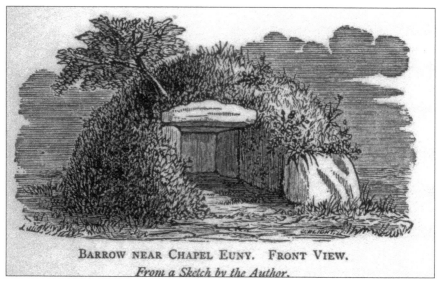

BARROW NEAR CHAPEL EUNY. FRONT VIEW.
*From a Sketch by the Author.*

Sketch of the Chapel Euny passage grave, drawn by Borlase and illustrated in his *Naenia Cornubiae* of 1872.

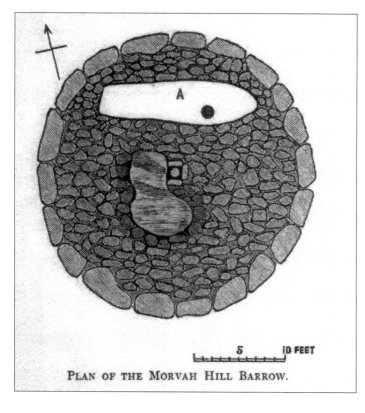

PLAN OF THE MORVAH HILL BARROW.

Plan of the Morvah Hill kerbed cairn dug by Borlase in 1863, one of 'upward of two hundred' claimed by him as opened in the Duchy, most of which have no surviving record.

further paper on Cornish barrows in *Archaeologia* 49 (1885), and continued his diggings well into the 1880s.

Borlase was a complex and interesting character about whom too little is known. He travelled widely, visiting the United States and Japan in 1875. In 1880 he was elected Liberal MP for East Cornwall, and when the seat was divided in 1885 he subsequently represented St Austell. The following year he was made Parliamentary Secretary to the Local Government Board. However by this time his taste for the high life was driving him into debt, and the resulting scandal, revealed by his disaffected Portuguese mistress, brought him to bankruptcy. He resigned his seat and apparently went to Ireland as a remittance man, though he is also recorded as managing tin mines in the Iberian Peninsula.

Throughout his later life Borlase, despite his pecuniary problems, had no difficulty in publishing weighty works. In 1895 the produced a monograph on early Christianity in Cornwall, and two years later a three volume study of the dolmens of Ireland. Disowned by his family, he died in Bloomsbury at the early age of 51, and his somewhat disreputable life would be well worth a biography. Despite his failings, his contribution to the early history of his native county, however imperfect, must carry some redemption.

# BOYD DAWKINS, Sir William (1837–1929).

Sir William Boyd Dawkins (1837–1929), geologist and cave-explorer, whose penchant for self-publicity helped to popularise archaeology, particularly the earliest epochs.

Sir William Boyd Dawkins was born at Welshpool, Powys, in December 1837, son of a vicar, and was educated at Oxford. With a first class degree in natural sciences he developed an interest in geology and prehistory and undertook a dig at a hyena den at Wookey Hole in Somerset, the origin of his lifetime interest in extinct mammalia. A scholarship enabled him to study geology, and between 1861 and 1869 he was a member of the Geological Survey of Great Britain.

In 1869 Boyd Dawkins was appointed curator of natural history at Manchester Museum, then a neglected institution. In 1872 he became the first lecturer in geology at Owens College, being appointed professor two years later and occupying the chair until retirement in 1908. He continued his researches into early man and English fossil mammals, and between 1875 and 1878 he helped direct explorations at the cave systems of Creswell Crags in north-east Derbyshire. His associates were the Revd Magens Mello and Thomas Heath, curator of Derby Museum. Although their work provided further proof that man was a contemporary of the mammoth, it was marred by controversy.

Robin Hood's Cave provided a rare example of Palaeolithic British art, a horse's head carved on bone, but the tooth of a sabre-toothed cat was felt by Heath to have been illicitly introduced. Church Hole and Mother Grundy's

Boyd Dawkins helped to direct explorations at Creswell Crags, north-east Derbyshire, in the 1870s. Here piled-up spoil marks the digging-out of the Pin Hole, site of Neanderthal occupation of the gorge.

In Robin Hood's Cave the 1870s explorers found this carving of a horse's head on a piece of reindeer rib, one of the few examples of ancient cave art to be found in England.

Parlour were also investigated, producing many artefacts and Pleistocene animal bones, now preserved at Manchester Museum.

Apart from a prolific output of papers, Boyd Dawkins wrote two books, *Cave Hunting* (1874) and *Early Man in Britain* (1880), the former described as 'a remarkably fine, learned and sober study.' A man of great energy, he was described as 'at his best in the open air, at some such place as Arbor Low (the Derbyshire henge) which, with vivid imagination, he could people with the men of prehistoric times.' He also travelled widely, to the continent, America and Australia, and became drawn in the 1880s to engineering and industrial geology, becoming adviser and consultant to several industries.

It has been said that Boyd Dawkins had a weakness for the limelight of archaeological discovery. A great self-publicist, he indulged in a number of acrimonious arguments that were fully reported in the press. He was awarded the Lyell and Prestwich medals by the Geological Society, and was knighted in 1919. Made wealthy by his consultancies, he died in January 1929, bequeathing his books and many papers to Buxton Museum where a replica of his study was later established.

# BUCKLAND, William (1784–1856).

William Buckland
(1784–1856), geologist,
cave explorer, churchman
and complete eccentric who
sadly developed mental
problems in later life.

A complete eccentric, once described as 'one of the most extraordinary of Oxford's many extraordinary characters' William Buckland was born in March 1784, at Axminster, Devon, son of a rector. His interest in geology and natural history was aroused by boyhood rambles examining the quarries of his native county. He was educated at Winchester College and Oxford, graduating in classics and theology in 1804. He was ordained priest in 1808 and spent much time gathering rocks and fossils in midland and south-western England, the nucleus of a later museum collection.

In 1813 Buckland was appointed reader in mineralogy at Oxford and became the first ever professor of geology six years later. He convinced himself that geological facts were consistent with the Biblical record of a 'universal deluge' which he equated with Noah's flood. His lectures were both popular and well-attended, his eccentricities legion (his umbrella was engraved 'stolen from Dr Buckland') and his fame spread as a result of his investigation of fossil cave faunas. In 1821 he dug at Kirkdale Cavern, Yorkshire, where his discovery of a variety of bones from many extinct species such as elephant, rhinoceros and hippopotamus excited much interest as he was able to prove they were prey or carrion brought in by hyenas and therefore part of the local fauna. The results of the dig were published in his *Reliquiae Diluvianae* of 1823.

Buckland's Oxford lectures were popular and well-attended. Here, in 1823, surrounded by a variety of fossils, he dilates on the mandible of some extinct species.

In 1821 Buckland dug at Paviland Cave on the Gower Peninsular. This cross-section shows the bones of the so-called 'Red Lady' below the man on the ladder. Note also Buckland's little dog at far left, and the climber clinging on to the rock face at top right.

That same year Buckland dug at Paviland or Goat's Hole Cave on the Gower in south Wales, disinterring the part remains of a human skeleton he called the Red Lady from the red ochre stained bones, which he dismissed as those of a camp follower from the local Roman garrison. The bones were actually those of a late Palaeolithic hunter, now claimed to be the oldest fossil human remains ever discovered. Buckland also wrote the first scientific paper describing a dinosaur found at Stonesfield which he christened *Megalosaurus*.

In 1825, possibly short of funds, Buckland was considering leaving Oxford, but he secured a canonry of Christ Church, with a house, generous stipend and no duties. He then married, and for the next twenty years enjoyed increasing fame and achievement. His new home overflowed with geological specimens and a whole menagerie of exotic pets. His dinner parties were notorious for the bizarre dishes he concocted, his avowed ambition being to eat his way through the animal kingdom.

A contemporary described Buckland as 'cheery, humorous, bustling, full of eloquence with which he too blended much true wit.' He invariably carried his famous blue bag, stuffed with the latest finds which he described to the amusement of his audience. Some of his peers deplored his showmanship and lack of gravitas, commenting that 'many grave people thought our science was altered to buffoonery by an Oxford Don.' However his achievements were considerable. He was a founder member of the Zoological Society of London, a leading light of the Geological Society, a fellow of the Royal Society and president of the British Association for the Advancement of Science in 1832.

In 1845, dissatisfied with the Oxford academic scene Buckland secured the appointment of Dean of Westminster, but by 1850 signs of a severe mental breakdown became marked, perhaps resulting from a fall from a coach. He was unable to perform his duties as dean or professor and was eventually placed in a mental asylum at Clapham where he died in August 1856.

For a hundred years after his death Buckland was dismissed as a capricious figure attempting unsuccessfully to reconcile geology with the Bible. It now seems clear he was in fact a leading light in the new era of geology who made the science acceptable to the Oxford Anglican establishment.

# CAMDEN, William (1551–1623).

William Camden (1551–1623) the most important of England's early antiquarian writers.

Perhaps the greatest of England's early antiquaries, William Camden was born in London in May 1551, son of a painter and stainer. A student at Oxford, he became involved in a religious dispute and was not awarded a degree. Many years later when his fame was assured, the university offered him an MA, which he refused, having as he put it 'established his reputation upon a better bottom.'

A long-serving master of Westminster School, Camden spent many years traversing the nation seeking material for a large-scale work on British history and topography. Sponsored among others by the poet Sir Philip Sidney, he considerably widened the scope of John Leland's earlier index of antiquities in his unpublished *Itinerary*, covering virtually the whole period from prehistoric times onwards. His mass of accumulated facts was eventually published in Latin in his *Britannia* of 1586, a work inspired by the geographer and mapmaker Abraham Ortelius who persuaded him to begin a written account of his researches in 1577. His perambulations included traversing most of Hadrian's Wall in 1599, though he avoided Housesteads and its notorious robber gang.

The volume was a monumental work, especially noteworthy when one considers the age of the author. It became the first English archaeological best-seller and was influential as a reference work for over 200 years. The book went through five Latin editions before the first English one was published in 1610. Some of its entries still remain valid for reference purposes even today. Like his predecessor Leland, Camden was unable to distinguish the builders of the more ancient field monuments which received mention even though the work was conceived as a history of Roman Britain. Such sites were credited to the 'British', the Saxons or Danes, and many were interpreted as the result of sanguinary conflicts between any combination of the three.

Camden noted the existence of early races before the time of Julius Caesar, but was unable to say anything positive about a period so remote in time. In fact, as a classical scholar well-versed in Latin texts, he could only advance the limited view that pre-Roman Britain was inhabited by shadowy 'aboriginals' about whom no useful facts could be gleaned. Camden of course gained many laurels in other spheres outside the scope of this narrative, and died in Chiselhurst, Kent in November 1623.

# CARRINGTON, Samuel (1798–1870).

Samuel Carrington (1798–1870), geologist, village schoolmaster and inveterate barrow-digger on behalf of his patron, Thomas Bateman.

Forever identified archaeologically with Thomas Bateman the Derbyshire antiquary, Samuel Carrington was born at Wetton, Staffordshire in November 1798, the son of a mine-captain at Ecton copper mine. At the age of twenty-one he emigrated to America, but was soon home, vowing 'to never quit again his native parish.' He became master of Wetton School and served as parish clerk as well as keeping a smallholding in the village.

A man of remarkable mental and physical energy, Carrington met Bateman in 1845 and on his behalf opened over 100 burial mounds, mainly in the area around Wetton. The contents of the tumuli were passed on to his employer, together with detailed reports of the openings, sent in a series of letters. His excavations form a complete section in Bateman's *Ten Years' Diggings* (1861). Carrington continued his barrow digging after his patron's death with John Fossick Lucas (1838–1872) of Fenny Bentley, who dug several Derbyshire cairns but regrettably left few records of his openings.

In 1864-5 Carrington directed the clearance of Thor's Cave, Wetton, producing evidence of prehistoric, Romano-British and Anglian occupation. He also dug over the site of a Romano-British farmstead at Wetton, regarding it somewhat tongue-in-cheek as a 'North Staffordshire Pompeii.' He ranged

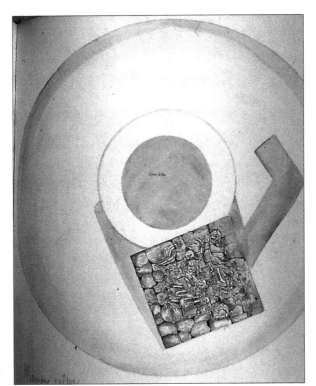

Carrington was a keen observer, and his plan of the Brown's Low barrow, North Staffordshire, clearly shows a prehistoric exposure platform with sundry disarticulated bones on display. The mound interior had been destroyed by a limekiln.

Carrington's grave in Wetton churchyard was designed by Gilbert Scott and displays examples of the rare fossils he discovered on the surrounding Mountain Limestone.

widely over the Carboniferous limestone around his home, collecting thousands of geological specimens over the years. Six of the species were the first ever identified locally, and four were named either after him or his native village.

As well as contributing papers to local societies, Carrington wrote a curious and instructive manuscript play called *The Barrow-Digger's Restitution of the Lost Archives of Ancient Britain,* embellished with sketches of barrows, artefacts and cartoons relating to the work which is centred around Wetton, the main characters being Bateman and Carrington himself.

Carrington died in October 1870 and was buried at Wetton. In 1874 a public subscription led to the erection of a tombstone over his grave, designed by Gilbert Scott. It is decorated with fossils native to the district, including the six types he first discovered. He was fittingly described by Charles Roach Smith as 'a very intelligent man; a good geologist; and an enthusiastic excavator of tumuli. Seldom are such men appreciated; and I fear he was not an exception from the common fate of the worthy, unselfish poor.'

# CUNNINGTON, Edward (1825–1916).

Edward Cunnington (1825–1916), once disparagingly dismissed as 'a local Schliemann' was a great nephew of the extensive barrow-digger William, friend and companion of Sir Richard Hoare.

Edward Cunnington, born in Weymouth, Dorset, in 1825, was a great nephew of William Cunnington who dug several hundred barrows on behalf of his patron, Sir Richard Hoare. During his long lifetime he opened some 53 tumuli around Dorchester and Weymouth, many of them along the Dorset Ridgeway. Printed reports exist of only a few including the Clandon Barrow and Ridgeway No. 7 both of which revealed rich gravegoods. However in old age he wrote up the accounts of his other digs in a manuscript notebook which survives, together with watercolour plans, illustrations, sections and gravegoods, in Dorset County Museum.

Cunnington achieved fame in Thomas Hardy's writings as the model for his elderly and unethical antiquary in his short story *A Tryst at an Ancient Earthwork,* where the writer described him as:

'A man about sixty, small in figure, with grey old-fashioned whiskers cut to the shape of a pair of crumb-brushes. He is entirely in black broadcloth – or rather, at present, black and brown, for he is bespattered with mud from his heels to the crown of his low hat. He has no consciousness of this – no sense of anything but his purpose, his ardour for which causes his eyes to shine like those of a lynx, and gives his motions all the elasticity of an athlete's.'

One of Cunnington's targets was the Clandon Barrow, a prominent landmark near Maiden Castle in Dorset. It covered a series of burials, though its base was never penetrated.

This fine gold breastplate, similar to one found by William Cunnington in the Bush barrow, was discovered by Edward Cunnington, with a bronze dagger, amber cup and shale mace-head deep in the tumulus.

The story presents a picture of illicit digging at the Roman temple built on the site of the earlier Maiden Castle hill-fort, resulting in the purloining of a gold statuette of the goddess Minerva, now in Dorset Museum. Elsewhere Hardy described Cunnington somewhat sardonically as 'a local Schliemann,' a reference to the explorer of ancient Troy, whose activities were not always beyond reproach.

Cunnington's work appears reasonable for its time, with descriptions of barrow structures, preservation of artefacts and other gravegoods and commentaries on the burials whose bones were often examined by experts such as John Thurnam. The greatest pity is that his manuscript, together with the accompanying illustrative material, has never been published. Cunnington died in his native Weymouth in 1916.

# CUNNINGTON, William (1754–1810).

William Cunnington (1754–1810), merchant and Sir Richard Hoare's great friend, on whose behalf he opened some 465 burial mounds in Wiltshire and Dorset.

William Cunnington was born at Gretton, Northamptonshire in 1754, son of a draper. His father apprenticed him to a draper in Warminster, Wiltshire and by 1775 he had settled at Heytesbury where he established a thriving business as a mercer, draper and wool merchant. He married in 1787 and his three daughters subsequently aided him in copying up his antiquarian writings and arranging his archaeological finds.

For the last twenty years of his life Cunnington suffered from severe headaches, perhaps a result of the acromegaly which slowly developed over those years. His doctor told him 'I must ride out or die – I preferred the former, and thank God, though poorly, I am yet alive.' During his perambulations he observed the barrow cemeteries prevalent in the Wessex landscape, and from 1800, encouraged by various local savants, began to explore them. One of his advisers, the Revd Thomas Leman, observed that Cunnington was 'certainly a very clever man, but without the advantages of a learned education.' Another acquaintance wrote that he 'displayed very considerable powers of mind, as well as originality . . . and left us in admiration of acquirements so rarely met with in men of his rank and calling.'

In 1801 Cunnington was elected FSA, and two years later was introduced to Sir Richard Hoare, the wealthy owner of Stourhead who was planning a history of his native county. On his behalf, and assisted with a corps of full-time diggers, Cunnington opened over 450 burial mounds, mainly in Wiltshire, and including long barrows as well as round. Among the most spectacular in

To mark his openings Cunnington deposited lead squares stamped with his initials and the date of excavation in the barrows he investigated, a practice inherited from William Stukeley, whose own tokens he occasionally found.

The Bush Barrow on Normanton Down, Wiltshire, was dug by Cunnington in 1808, revealing a rich Bronze Age burial with gold artefacts.

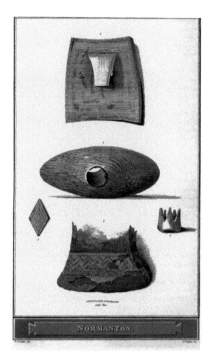

Hoare's *Ancient Wiltshire* embodies plates showing the finds from the Bush Barrow. This illustration depicts the gold belt fastening (top), a perforated fossil stone pebble macehead, and part of a dagger-handle, set with hundreds of tiny gold pins.

finds were the Bush Barrow at Normanton, the Upton Lovel 'Gold barrow' and several in the Winterborne Stoke group. He sent details of the excavations in a series of letters to his patron; his daughters transcribed copies which were later bound into three volumes, now held by the Wiltshire Archaeological Society. All the finds were displayed in a purpose-built museum, the Moss House, erected in his garden. After his death Hoare purchased the relics which are now housed in Devizes Museum.

The first part of Hoare's *Ancient History of Wiltshire* (1812) was dedicated to Cunnington as a tribute to his pioneering and well-documented work, which included the investigation of several ancient settlements, and his extensive collection. Cunnington also collected minerals and fossils, gathering a fine series of samples for the geologist William Smith. Cunnington was criticised by later Nineteenth century archaeologists for his *modus operandi* which included barrow-openings by the central shaft method, and his attitude to finds (skeletal remains were not removed, nor were imperfect pottery vessels and certain small finds). Nevertheless his work made an important contribution to the methodology of barrow-digging, both in recording and categorization, but the greatest achievement was in the gathering and publication of archaeological evidence, the watchword being 'We speak from facts, not theory.'

Cunnington died at Heytesbury in December 1810 from the slow, debilitating effects of his illness, sadly not able to view the first part of the printed history his work had done so much to bring to fruition.

# DAVIS, Joseph Barnard (1801–1881).

Joseph Barnard Davis (1801–81),
Staffordshire doctor and craniologist,
whose friendship with John Thurnam led
to *Crania Britannica* (1865), a study of
ancient British skullforms.

Joseph Barnard Davis was born in York in June 1801, son of a draper, and studied for the medical profession. At the age of nineteen he signed on as a surgeon on a Whitby whaler bound for the Arctic. He qualified LSA in 1823 and settled with his wife in Shelton, Staffordshire, where he lived for the rest of his life in a house that later became so crowded with cranial specimens that the locals referred to it as the 'Skullery.'

Appointed medical officer for Stoke-on-Trent, and parish medical officer for Shelton, Davis spent the rest of his working life in this relative backwater, devoting himself to his patients and his interests. His main obsession was craniology and he gradually accumulated a vast number of fully documented skulls and skeletons relating to the various races of man. In 1849 he visited the museum of Thomas Bateman, who became a lifelong friend; Bateman offered his collection of crania for Davis to put to 'some scientific account' and other assemblages were also made available for comparative purposes. He believed that important information could be extracted from the measurement and examination of skulls, and became an early member of the Ethnological and Anthropological societies.

In 1856 Davis and Dr John Thurnam began work on their *Crania Britannica,* a work published in a series of 'decades' each describing ten skulls, and completed in 1865. The pair gathered much skeletal information, mostly gleaned from excavations in British barrows, and seen as representational of the races making up the island population. Davis's own assemblage of crania was published in 1867 as *Thesaurus Craniorum,* a copious reference work which included all the items in his burgeoning collection. In fact he spared neither time, money or labour in gathering specimens, conducting a truly monumental correspondence with antiquaries, collectors, travellers and foreigners in the pursuit of his enthusiasm.

Elected FRS in 1868, Davis was a joint editor of the *Journal of Anthropology* and *Anthropologia.* By the end of his life he had joined over thirty medical, scientific and anthropological societies across the world, contacts which gave him information and the opportunity to publish his own work and ideas. After the death of his first wife, he remarried, at the age of 77, a lady 50 years his junior, an act that led to the estrangement of his son Joseph. Davis died at Shelton in May 1881, having made a valuable contribution to the study of the material remains of Britain's early races.

# DENISON (formerly Conyngham), Albert, first Baron Londesborough (1805–1860).

Denison, Lord Albert (1805–60), once described as 'like a comb, all teeth and backbone' was a fabulously wealthy collector and excavator, and the first president of the British Archaeological Association.

Albert Denison was an imposing figure, some six foot four inches in height, tall, dark and slim and 'like a comb, all teeth and backbone.' He was born Albert Conyngham in London in October 1805, son of a marquess. He served as an army officer between 1820 and 1824, but resigned and joined the diplomatic service, where his work was so appreciated that he was created KCH in 1829 at the precocious age of twenty-three! He later served as Liberal MP for Canterbury but in March 1850 was created Baron Londesborough in the East Riding of Yorkshire. The previous year he had altered his name to Denison to comply with the provisions of his uncle's will, and to enable him to inherit the latter's vast estates and even vaster wealth.

An enthusiastic antiquary, Londesborough was elected FSA in 1840 and FRS ten years later. He was first president of the BAA in 1843, but resigned in 1849 after a disagreement with the hierarchy of the society, subsequently becoming a vice-president of the rival Archaeological Institute. He was also a devotee of the turf, and a committed barrow-digger who excavated a substantial number of tumuli. His first explorations took place on his Kentish estates, where he and John Akerman pillaged numerous Anglo-Saxon burial mounds, followed by further incursions during the BAA Congress at Canterbury in 1843.

From the early 1850s onwards Londesborough commenced barrow-digging on his Yorkshire Wolds estates, examining long and round tumuli on Seamer

Lord Albert was involved in many barrow-digs, including this one in Kent in 1844 which was interrupted by an inconvenient rainstorm.

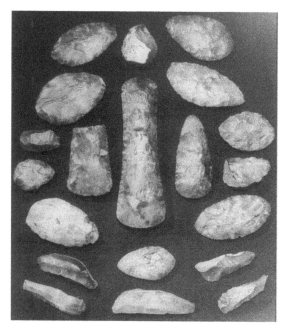

This fine collection of Neolithic flint tools was found by Denison in a long barrow on Seamer Moor near Scarborough.

Another interesting tumulus was opened at Kelleythorpe on the Yorkshire Wolds. The central interment was in a slab-built cist with a paved floor, and contained a crouched skeleton with a beaker, bronze dagger and a stone bracer embellished with four bronze gold-headed rivets.

Moor, followed by other examples on Willerby Wold and among the Driffield group at Kelleythorpe. In 1857 he tackled the huge Neolithic mound called Willey Howe near Wold Newton; despite a deep cutting little was found, though William Greenwell, who followed him thirty years later, located an inscribed stone slab left by the baronet. According to his fellow investigators, his expression 'vewy intewesting' was usually forthcoming whenever a noteworthy relic or burial was uncovered.

Londesborough's collections were extensive, wide-ranging and of high quality. They included silver plate, armour, furniture and paintings, but most were dispersed after his death. Apparently highly strung, he expected his servants to be invisible and never acknowledged their presence. His two marriages (his first wife dying in 1841) produced twelve children, though by the later 1850s poor health was undermining his constitution. In the winter of 1859, after spending much time at his villa in Cannes, he moved to the Sussex coast, but died in London in January 1860 at the early age of 54. He was buried in the family vault at Grimston, followed to his grave by some 400 tenants and tradesmen who came spontaneously to offer their respects to his memory.

# DOUGLAS, James (1753–1819).

James Douglas (1753–1819),
a soldier, cleric and inveterate
antiquary whose *Nenia Britannica*
of 1793 was the first published
work to describe the burial customs
of the Pagan Anglo-Saxons.

James Douglas, son of an innkeeper, was born in London in January 1753. His parents died young, and he was brought up by his elder brother William in Manchester. William, a cloth merchant, duly sent James to Italy as his agent, but dismissed him when he helped himself to funds entrusted to him. In desperation he joined the Austrian army as a cadet. The next few years remain obscure, but by 1777 he was back in England, and the following year was commissioned into the Leicestershire Militia, working as an engineer fortifying the Chatham Lines on the Medway against possible French attack.

Douglas's sappers cut through dozens of Anglo-Saxon burial mounds whilst reshaping the Chatham defences, and he amassed a collection of relics, even employing troops in opening graves during their off-duty hours, with the permission of their Colonel, Hugh Debbieg. He kept careful notes, sketches and illustrations of the burials and gravegoods the soldiers unearthed. In 1781 he translated the Frenchman Guibert's *General Essay on Military Tactics* into English, and the following year published anonymously *Travelling Anecdotes through Various Parts of Europe,* a successful venture which went through several editions. In 1783 he was elected FSA, joining a learned body 'that meant more to him than any other.' He was ordained that same year.

Douglas drew this light-hearted depiction of a barrow-dig around 1787, and it probably relates to a tumulus opened on Wimbledon Common. The artist himself wields a pickaxe as his helpers unearth an unlikely series of relics; note the individual sieving the soil and the little dog relieving himself in a handy vessel.

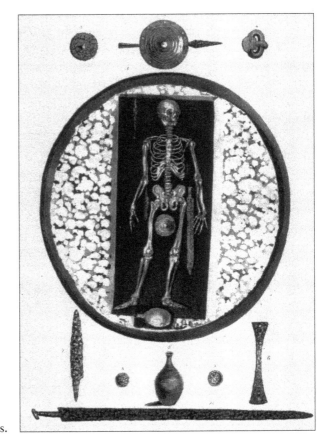

Probably the first ground plan of a barrow known to British archaeology, this is Tumulus 1 on the Chatham Lines, opened by Douglas in 1779, and depicts an Anglo-Saxon inhumation with his accompanying artefacts.

In 1785 Douglas produced *A Dissertation on the Antiquity of the Earth* distinguished by case studies, particularly fossils discovered by himself, which suggested to him that the earth had been peopled by animals and humans later destroyed by Noah's flood. At this time the vast duration of geological time was unknown, but his concluding remarks showed that the fossils he had collected lived where they were found, though in a tropical climate. To Douglas a forty-day flood could not have transported the remains any great distance, and he believed the earth itself had some means of preserving organic remains. Though Douglas was not a lone voice in reaching these conclusions, they were nevertheless of far-reaching intellectual significance.

However, Douglas's main claim to antiquarian fame was his *Nenia Britannica*, a sepulchral history of Britain from the earliest times to the advent of Christianity. He published the great tome in twelve parts between 1786–1793, and as a bound volume in the latter year, with numerous illustrations etched by himself. The work, a general history of British funerary customs from prehistoric times onwards, was beset with problems and delays, and was poorly received simply because it was way ahead of its time; not until 1835 was its true merit appreciated.

Douglas hoped the book would help repair his ailing fortunes, but not only did it fail to do this, but his eyes suffered from the fumes given off by the acid used in engraving the copper plates for the illustrations, and his general constitution also faltered under remittent colds and fevers. In later years he met Hoare and Cunnington, accompanying them on barrow-digging forays, and corresponded with antiquaries such as Godfrey Faussett and Hayman Rooke.

Douglas also tried his hand at novels, of which he published three, one of which has no surviving copies. He was also a talented painter in oils and miniature, and an accomplished engraver. In later life he ministered at various livings, finally serving as chaplain to the 10th Royal Hussars at Preston barracks, Chatham, where he died of a chill in November 1819. His collection was presented to the Ashmolean Museum, Oxford, where it now reposes. His epitaph in St Peter's Church, Preston, records 'he has most learnedly explained all that relates to the burial of the early inhabitants of Britain' concluding fittingly 'He was a disturber, though not without reverence, of other men's sepulchres. May he, in his own, rest quietly.'

# EVANS, Sir John (1823–1908).

Sir John Evans (1823–1908), here shown with fashionable facial fuzz. Somewhat of a dandy when young, he was a manufacturer, numismatist and collector who wrote the first definitive texts on British stone and bronze implements, and pre-Roman coins.

Sir John Evans was born in November 1823 at Burnham, Buckinghamshire, son of a schoolmaster and cleric. His father encouraged him in the study of numismatics and fossils, and sent him and his brother to Germany in 1839 to study the language. He intended to enter Oxford but his uncle offered him employment in paper manufacturing which became his lifelong career. Eventually he ran the mills and built up the fortunes of the firm.

Evans's earliest enthusiasm was coinage, though he gained his election as FSA (at the precocious age of twenty-nine) by a report on a Roman villa he dug at Boxmoor. Digging never loomed large in his life and he was always more of a synthesiser of information relating to the past. Nevertheless he took part in an enthusiastic day's plundering of an Iron Age cemetery at Halstatt, Austria, in 1866, and in the mid-1860s accompanied Canon William Greenwell in barrow openings on the Yorkshire Wolds.

He also shared in editing the *Numismatic Chronicle* and in 1859 visited France with Joseph Prestwich, where the pair inspected the vast collection of Palaeolithic stone tools found by Frenchman Boucher de Perthes in the Somme gravels. He felt the artefacts belonged to an era 'remote beyond any of which we have hitherto found traces' and had no doubt as to their authenticity. He became an expert in flint knapping and was for a time nicknamed 'Flint' Evans,

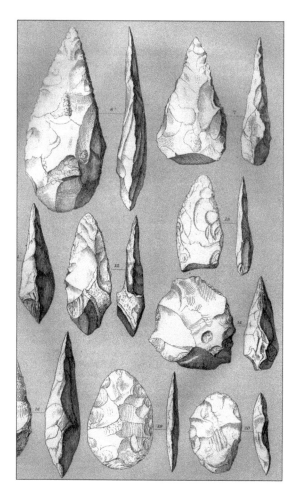

This illustration, taken from *Archaeologia* 39 (1861), depicts a series of Palaeolithic tools found in the 'Drift' and drawn from collections held by Evans and his friends.

This fine bronze medallion, showing a bearded Evans in later life, was presented to him in 1887 by the Numismatic Society in recognition of his outstanding achievements in the study of coinage.

his work receiving praise from that arch-faker Edward Simpson, the notorious 'Flint Jack.' In 1862 he was elected FRS on the strength of his researches.

In 1863 Evans published *The Coins of the Ancient Britons*, described as a 'revolutionary and ground-breaking opus' and a standard reference text for nearly 100 years. He then turned his attention to stone implements, visiting the classic French cave sites and becoming an acknowledged expert on the subject. In 1872 *The Ancient Stone Implements, Weapons and Ornaments of Great Britain* established a classification of such objects, establishing the sequence and typology of lithic implement forms.

Evans worked himself hard in later life; as well as running his expanding paper mills, he undertook many professional duties, plus those related to his archaeological and numismatic interests. He went on to classify British bronzes in his 1881 volume *Ancient Bronze Implements,* another notable study in evolution by form and series and another significant contribution to implement classification by someone whose study and research was essentially part-time.

Evans retired from business in 1885. He married three times, his first wife dying young after producing five children, including Sir Arthur Evans, the excavator of Minoan Crete. His second marriage was childless, and his third, in 1892, was to a lady 33 years his junior; the union took place shortly after his knighthood and the couple were blessed with one daughter. Evans died in May 1908 loaded with honours and was buried at Abbot's Langley. Some of his collection went to the British Museum, other sections to the John Evans room at the Ashmolean Museum, Oxford. John Evans's great contributions in many spheres of intellectual activity still arouse our admiration of someone whose sheer breadth of learning was truly outstanding.

# FAUSSETT, Bryan (1720–1776).

Bryan Faussett (1720–76), cleric, numismatist and inveterate barrow-digger, who opened some 777 Anglo-Saxon tumuli in Kent during his busy lifetime.

Bryan Faussett was born in October 1720 at Heppington, near Canterbury, Kent, eldest of thirteen children. His early interest in antiquarianism was aroused at the age of ten when he witnessed Cromwell Mortimer, once described as an 'impertinent, assuming, empiric physician' opening Saxon barrows on Chartham Down in east Kent. Faussett was educated at Oxford where he shared his father's Jacobite sympathies and attempted to raise a volunteer force in support of Prince Charles. He was also rusticated for smuggling a prostitute into his rooms, and was later refused a fellowship at All Souls for failing to be a person of 'chaste and virtuous life.' However, his appeal was successful and after two years he was given a living in Shropshire. He married and returned to Kent on his father's death, succeeding to the family estates on the death of his mother in 1761.

Despite his wealth Faussett felt slighted by the higher clergy and gentlemen of the county, though a friend commented that he 'does not long agree with anybody.' He also failed to obtain a benefice of his own until 1765 though, like Stephen Isaacson he may well have been regarded as 'by no means an ornament to the church' being dismissed as 'a man subject to passion, and to utter at such times very unclerical language.'

Breach Down in Kent, showing a cluster of Anglo-Saxon burial mounds, typical of those excoriated by Faussett. This particular Pagan cemetery was investigated by the British Archaeological Association in 1844.

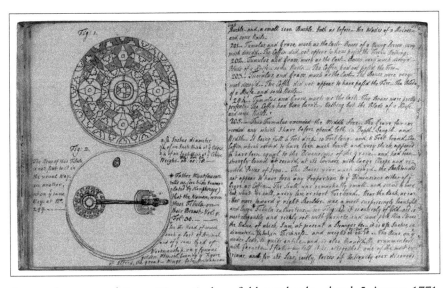

A page from one of Faussett's meticulous field notebooks, dated 5 August 1771, describes and illustrates the superb Kingston brooch, one of the most famous pieces of Saxon jewellery unearthed in Britain.

Fausset's first enthusiasms were heraldry, genealogy and numismatics, but a visit to Tremworth Down in 1757 to view a 'Roman' burial-ground, whetted his appetite to reinvestigate the site, and by the time of his death nineteen years later he had opened some 777 grave mounds on the east Kent downs. Though his explorations were large-scale, he failed to appreciate that the barrow clusters he worked at were Anglo-Saxon, referring to them as 'Britons Romanized.' However, for the time, his recording was precise and careful; written first in a field notebook and later transcribed into a narrative journal, he provided an exemplary account of the graves he uncovered, chronicling all grave-goods and sexing and ageing skeletons with much accuracy. His operations would now be condemned as hasty – on one day in July 1771 his workforce dug thirty-one tumuli in a day, a fortnight after opening nine barrows in two hours!

Faussett continued to direct barrow excavations even when gout forced him to watch operations from his coach. His greatest prize was the Kingston jewelled disc-brooch, found by his son Henry, 'born and bred an antiquary.' The youngster bore it proudly to his father, and the local rustics later reported that the carriage drove away with such a load of gold that the wheels could hardly turn! His collection represented the finest group of Anglo-Saxon antiquities until the discovery of the Sutton Hoo treasure.

Faussett died in February 1776 and was buried at Nackington. His great assemblage remained virtually unknown until 1844 when it was shown to the BAA members at their first congress at Canterbury. The British Museum declined to purchase the relics when they were put on sale, and they were bought by Joseph Mayer in 1855 who later presented them to Liverpool Museum. Charles Roach Smith edited Faussett's manuscript which was published in 1856 as *Inventorium Sepulchrale*. It remains an important and highly readable account of his activities, enlivened by his acid comments on the idlers who came to gawp at his diggings. It is perhaps regrettable that the great assemblage relating to Anglo-Saxon Kent is preserved not in its native county but some distance away in Lancashire.

# GREENWELL, William (1820–1918).

William Greenwell (1820–1918), polymath, churchman, extensive collector and even more extensive barrow-opener, who dug widely in England over many decades.

Described by John Evans as 'eminently unclerical in his manners and manner of thinking, and a very sensible man' William Greenwell was born in March 1820, appropriately at Greenwell Ford, near Lanchester, Co. Durham. His father was a deputy lieutenant of the county, and the Greenwells had been ensconced at the family seat for over 300 years. He studied at Durham University and intended to read for the bar, but ill-health forced him back to Durham where he studied theology. He gained his MA in 1843 and was ordained the following year, serving in various curacies before his ordination as a minor canon of Durham Cathedral in 1854. In 1862 he became cathedral librarian, and served in several secular capacities as a JP, Poor Law Guardian, County Alderman and an officer in the Durham Volunteers.

Apart from his major interests, archaeology, medieval manuscripts and fly fishing, Greenwell was a noted collector who amassed, by gift and purchase, large collections of prehistoric stone, flint and bronze implements and Greek coins. During his long lifetime he opened some 295 long and round barrows in a number of northern and southern counties of England. At one time General Pitt Rivers was 'his enthusiastic pupil.' He was also present at barrow openings with other noted diggers such as John Thurnam in Wiltshire, William Collings Lukis in Yorkshire (who drew many illustrations for Greenwell's later barrow book) and Llewellynn Jewitt in Derbyshire.

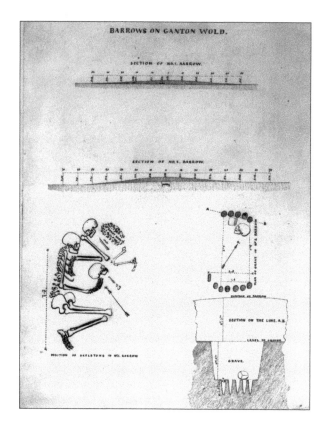

The Canon never drew plans and sections of the burial mounds he opened. This rare sheet showing tumuli opened by him on Ganton Wold, Yorkshire, in 1867 was the work of Pitt Rivers who dug with him during that season.

The largest mound tackled by Greenwell was Willy Howe, Wold Newton, first investigated by Lord Albert Denison in 1857. Greenwell's opening, thirty years later, proved as unproductive as that of his predecessor.

Most intriguing of Greenwell's finds was this trio of chalk drums found in a child's grave on Folkton Wold in 1889. The gravegoods are unique, and such items were probably more commonly made of wood or other less durable material.

Greenwell's first dig was in 1847, but he began his long campaign in 1864, reporting his finds first in *British Barrows* (1877), described with some justification as the dullest book ever written! This was followed by supplements in *Archaeologia* 52 and 60. Unfortunately he rarely recorded the structure of the mounds he dug and came into conflict with John Mortimer in the 1860s when the Yorkshireman accused him of missing sub-surface burials in wolds round barrows. Greenwell dismissed his rival as 'a scoundrel' and his conduct 'that of a rascal' but it seems clear the latter spoke with some justification. Later in the century the pair became reconciled, and collaborated in digs at the Iron Age barrow cemetery, the Danes' Graves, in East Yorkshire. Greenwell himself had no high opinion of other wolds diggers, once dismissing Thomas Kendall of Pickering as 'a person who has destroyed most of the barrows in his district.'

Greenwell opened a number of long barrows, mainly in the Cotswolds, often in association with George Rolleston (who reported on the skulls in *British Barrows*) and the Revd David Royce, vicar of Nether Swell. The Canon's considerable collection was sold or gifted to the British Museum during his lifetime, and though it represented a seminal assemblage of British prehistoric material, it was only properly catalogued as *The Greenwell Collection* in 1985. His crania were presented to the University Museum, Oxford. Elected FRS in 1878, Greenwell remained a keen angler until his death. He died in January 1918 at North Bailey, Durham, and was interred at Lanchester. Despite criticisms, he remains one of the outstanding barrow-diggers of the Nineteenth century.

# HOARE, Sir Richard Colt (1758–1838).

Sir Richard Colt Hoare (1758–1838), Wiltshire baronet whose enthusiasm for the ancient sites of his native county led to widespread barrow investigations and two iconic volumes on the subject.

Sir Richard Hoare was born at Barnes, Surrey, eldest son of a baronet and banker, and was destined for a career in banking. He married in 1783 but his wife died two years later; in the same year he inherited the Stourhead estate and henceforth devoted his life to his property and his interests. These included classical studies, literature and the arts. The death of his wife was a traumatic event and to assuage his grief he embarked on two grand tours of Europe, examining classical antiquities and collecting for his family seat. When the French Revolution compelled his return home he embarked on tours of Wales and Ireland, and subsequently determined to chronicle the early history of his adopted county, bringing a wide literary skill and an unrivalled experience in field observation and description to the task.

Hoare's meeting with William Cunnington in 1803 led him to propose a collaboration to produce a work on the ancient history of Wiltshire, with Cunnington leading a series of yearly digging campaigns organised by Hoare who selected the areas to explore. The main targets were the burial mounds which studded the downland, though 'British' villages and Roman sites were also subjected to the spade. Each season's work was planned like a military campaign and Cunnington wrote up descriptions of the digs and preserved the antiquities unearthed at his own home.

Hoare transcribed Cunnington's letters and in the published works made it appear as though he was personally present at each dig, though it was doubtful

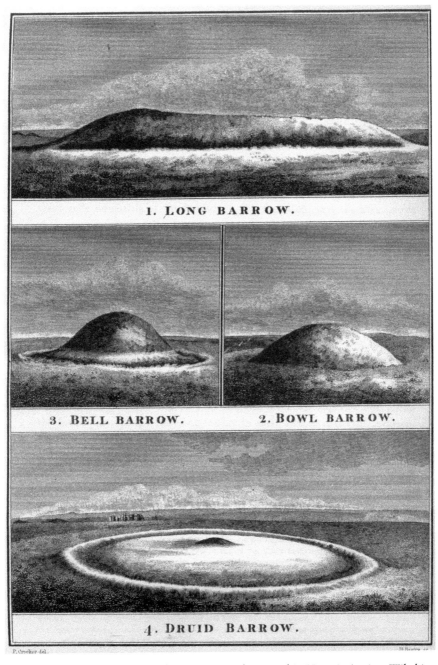

1. LONG BARROW.

3. BELL BARROW.    2. BOWL BARROW.

4. DRUID BARROW.

P. Crocker del.                    R. Rawles sc.

Drawings of barrow types found in Wessex, and pictured in Hoare's *Ancient Wiltshire*.

'Group of Barrows, south of Stone Henge,' an illustration *c.* 1806, showing Hoare and William Cunnington, left, supervising a dig perhaps undertaken by members of his permanent staff, Stephen and John Parker.

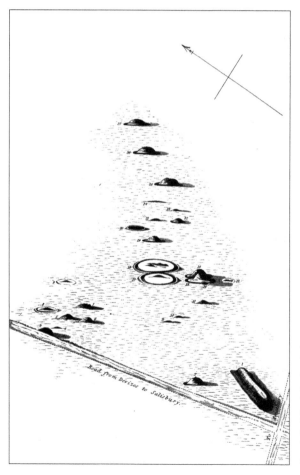

Road from Devizes to Salisbury.

A bird's-eye view of the barrow cemetery at Winterborne Stoke, extensively investigated by Hoare's workforce. Practically every type of barrow known in Wiltshire is represented in this group.

if this was the case. Some 465 tumuli were opened, including both long and round examples, and though he found it impossible to accurately date the monuments he remained in no doubt that 'the greater part of our Wiltshire barrows were the sepulchral monuments of the Celtic and first colonists of Britain.' The greater number of opened mounds had lead squares or circular brass medalets placed in excavated graves stamped with the initials of one or other of the pair, usually with the date included, an improvement on the practice initiated by William Stukeley who left current coins or tokens in the barrows he dug.

The first volume of *The Ancient History of Wiltshire*, dealing with the south of the county, appeared in 1812, and set a standard that was exemplary for the times. Though no plans or sections of excavated mounds were published, Hoare had many plans of barrow groups, hill forts and suchlike illustrated, plus a large scale plan of Salisbury Plain with every known barrow plotted and numbered. Many of the gravegoods were pictured in a series of full-page plates, and every barrow type found in Wiltshire was also depicted for the instruction of the uninitiated.

Hoare continued his researches into the Wiltshire barrows after Cunnington's death, though on a reduced scale. The second volume in the *Ancient History* series, published in 1819, dealt with the north of the county. The two works together represent the first of the great county archaeologies whose contents were constructed from systematic programmes of fieldwork and excavation. After Cunnington's death he purchased the relics culled from the Wiltshire graves from the family, and they were eventually passed on to the Wiltshire Archaeological Society's Museum at Devizes, a collection 'whose content has such a cardinal significance for Bronze Age archaeology.'

This is not the place to laud Hoare's other achievements in art, collecting or his development of the Stourhead estates. He followed his ancient history with one on modern Wiltshire, though as he aged he faced a series of ailments, including gout, rheumatism, migraines and deafness, foes he grappled with courageously until his death. Sir Richard died in May 1838 at his seat, and was buried in the family mausoleum at Stourton. More than anyone before him, he and his friend Cunnington had done much to lift the veil on England's ancient past.

# JEWITT, Llewellynn Frederick William (1816–1886).

Llewellynn Jewitt (1816–86), author, illustrator, publisher and barrow-digger, whose quarterly magazine *The Reliquary* was the first archaeologically based journal to be published in Britain.

Llewellynn Jewitt was a workaholic who once wrote 'mine has been (happily) a life of work and the words *holiday* and *rest* have ever been discarded from my dictionary as obsolete.' He was born at Kimberworth, south Yorkshire in November 1816, youngest of seventeen children of Arthur Jewitt, author and schoolmaster, and in 1818 the family moved to Duffield, near Derby. A writer and illustrator, he went to London in 1838, providing the drawings for many metropolitan publications. He had an antiquarian bent, joining the BAA in 1843, and in 1846 dug at a Roman villa at Headington, near Oxford. For a time he managed the illustrations for *Punch*, and in 1849 was appointed chief librarian of Plymouth Public Library, a post he held until 1853, during which time he was elected FSA.

In that year Jewitt moved to Derby where he started the *Derby Telegraph*, originally a monthly, but published as a penny weekly with the abolition of stamp duty. He remained its editor until 1868. Jewitt was a man of tremendous energy, who wrote on many subjects. He formed a local rifle corps in 1859, publishing a volume on rifle volunteers the following year, rejuvenated the moribund Derby County Museum, acting as honorary curator, and was employed by Thomas Bateman to illustrate all the artefacts gleaned from his many barrow excavations. In 1862 he commenced a series of barrow-diggings in the Derbyshire Peak on his own account, assisted by John Fossick Lucas

Jewitt investigated several Derbyshire tumuli, publishing accounts in his magazine, though his illustrations suggest the opening techniques leave something to be desired!

Jewitt produced numerous woodcuts of barrows, burials and artefacts such as this plan of a Thomas Bateman dig at a cairn in Monsal Dale in the Derbyshire Peak.

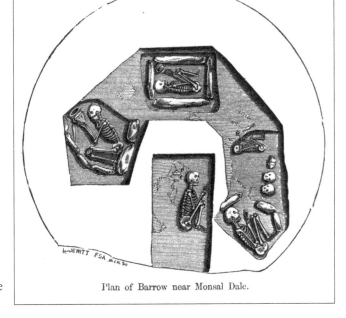

Plan of Barrow near Monsal Dale.

Jewitt and his wife lie buried in Winster churchyard; his tombstone is the weathered one on the left. On the right is the tomb of his son Llewellynn junior which bears a memorial to another son, Herbert, who was accidentally killed at sea in 1870.

and Samuel Carrington. Some of them were written up in his groundbreaking quarterly archaeological magazine *The Reliquary*, which he founded in 1860. He was its editor until his death in 1886, and the periodical thrived well into the twentieth century.

Jewitt's writings were legion, encompassing British ceramics, which he collected assiduously, guidebooks, topographical works and biographies. He published two archaeological books, *Grave Mounds and their Contents* (1870) and *Half-Hours with some English Antiquities* (1877), both replete with numerous woodcuts, and mines of information for their period. In 1868 Jewitt moved to Winster, deep in the Derbyshire Peak, where he knew much tragedy with the death of one of his sons at sea, and another of a fever, both within ten months of each other.

In 1880 Jewitt moved back to Duffield, where his much loved wife died in 1886. After this blow his life lost its purpose, and he followed her a few weeks later, being laid to rest alongside her in Winster churchyard. His friend William Henry Goss wrote his biography, *The Life and Death of Llewellynn Jewitt* in 1889, a turgid, rambling epistle 600 pages long, but a fascinating mine of information on the man and his times.

# LELAND, John (1503–1552).

John Leland (1503–52), earliest of the Tudor antiquaries, who 'though learned' was dismissed as 'a boaster.' Nevertheless his *Itinerary* did contain some nuggets of somewhat discursive archaeological merit.

John Leland was born in London in September 1503. His parents died young, and he was adopted, gaining his education at St Paul's School and Oxford. He was a poet and scholar who took holy orders, and after a spell with the Howard family, became librarian to Henry VIII and a royal chaplain. In 1533 he was appointed to a unique office, becoming the one and only 'King's Antiquary' with a commission to search the length and breadth of England and Wales for surviving antiquities and monuments of all kinds. His brief included a Royal command to 'peruse and diligently to serche' all monastic and college libraries for information on the remains of the past. His resulting tour of the realm took place between 1534–1543, during which, by his own account, he spared neither labour or cost in seeking his objectives.

Though dismissed by certain contemporaries as vainglorious and that 'though learned he was a boaster' Leland showed a remarkable industry in accumulating facts and was a close observer. His resulting, unpublished *Itinerary* includes, as well as remains, other objects of interest likely to stir the historian. He assiduously described Roman, Saxon and 'Danish' vestiges, yet showed little interest in either chronology or Pre-Roman Britain, though his excursions on Salisbury Plain recorded 'sepultures of men of warre' whilst making no mention of Stonehenge. He also noted 'pottes . . . digged out of the groundes in the feldes' though they were dismissed as Roman. Of the sites he visited he commented 'I hauve seen them; and noted yn doing so a hole worlde of things very memorable.'

These casual and imperfect gleanings helped establish a tradition whose path was enthusiastically trodden by many successors. His undertaking was extraordinarily ambitious, and marked the beginning of English topographical studies. Sadly it was recorded in 1549 that Leland had fallen insane some three years previously and in 1551 his brother was granted custody of his person and property. His illness may well have been a manic-depressive one, and it probably caused his death in April 1552. He was buried in the parish of Michael-le-Querne but a monument, said to have existed in the church was destroyed in the great fire of 1666.

# LUKIS, Frederick Corbin (1788–1871)

Frederick Corbin Lukis (1788–1871), polymath, antiquary and collector, who was a pioneer archaeologist in his native Channel Islands and England.

Frederick Lukis was born in February 1788 at St Peter Port, Guernsey, son of an officer in the local militia, who had also been a successful privateer and wine merchant. As a young man he became interested in a variety of disciplines and was commissioned an officer in the Guernsey Militia, eventually rising to the rank of lieutenant colonel. His interest in archaeology arose from visits to local chambered tombs, especially L'Ancresse Common where soldiers digging a redoubt stumbled across the entrance, disturbing pottery and bones. He began to discover, record and investigate the remains of Guernsey's heritage, writing in 1837 that he was 'determined to begin the excavation of the prehistoric remains of the Channel Islands.' As time passed he extended his barrow digging activities to England, opening burial mounds in Wiltshire and Norfolk. He often drew plans and sections of the sites he dug, many attractively coloured or tinted.

Lukis impressed the Derbyshire antiquary Thomas Bateman with his ideas on methods of interment in chambered barrows, and also pioneered the idea of distribution maps for recording artefacts. He made meticulous notes on his investigations and fieldwork in his *Collectanea Antiqua*, a handwritten archive bound into six volumes now preserved in Guernsey Museum, a body of work indispensable for any study of the island's prehistoric past. He also visited the ancient monuments in Brittany which are also described in his opus.

Neolithic chambered barrows particularly interested Lukis, who is seen here examining pottery sherds found at Le Creux es Faies L'Eree on his native Guernsey.

Lukis drew meticulous plans and sections of the sites he worked at, including this painting of the interior of the La Varde chamber, opened in 1837, though the depiction of the burials and gravegoods seems somewhat imaginative!

In 1853 Lukis was elected FSA for his meticulous research; of his six sons, two of whom died in their 'teens, several dabbled in archaeology, and one, William Collings, became a committed barrow-digger. Lukis was also interested in geology and local natural history, and his collection is likewise housed in Guernsey Museum. He died in November 1871 in Guernsey, recording in his will that his collection should be bequeathed to the states of Guernsey, a request honoured by his last surviving son, Francis Dubois, who died in 1907.

# LUKIS, William Collings (1817–1892).

William Collings Lukis (1817–92), third son of Frederick, was a churchman-archaeologist who dug tumuli principally in Wiltshire and Yorkshire.

William Lukis, third son of Frederick Corbin Lukis, was born in April 1817 in Guernsey. He was educated at Cambridge and took holy orders in 1841. Known for his 'tall, erect manly form, and genial countenance' he became a scholar of European fame, who served in three Wiltshire livings between his ordination and 1861 during which time he dug into a barrow group on Cow Down, opening seventeen tumuli and publishing a plan of the cemetery and several of the mounds he trenched. His report on the excavations shows an orderly method and concise description of the burials, though his investigations of several of the tumuli appear somewhat limited in scope.

Lukis later opened several long barrows in Wessex before his removal to Wath, near Ripon in 1862 where he resided until his death. In the 1860s he investigated a number of burial mounds around the Thornborough henges, work which was again conscientiously published, and assisted Canon Greenwell in uncovering Anglian interments from a cemetery in Yorkshire. He also drew many of the pottery vessels for the Canon's *British Barrows*, the latter remarking 'I am sure the labour was one of love.' Lukis knew several other noted archaeologists, including William Copeland Borlase, with who he collaborated on *The Rude Stone Monuments of Cornwall*, published in 1885.

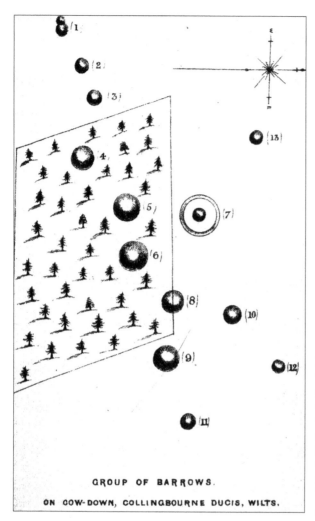

GROUP OF BARROWS.

ON COW-DOWN, COLLINGBOURNE DUCIS, WILTS.

Like his father, William worked with purpose and system as this plan of a barrow group on Cow Down, Wiltshire shows. He investigated many mounds in this cemetery, recording their opening in the *Wiltshire Archaeological Magazine*.

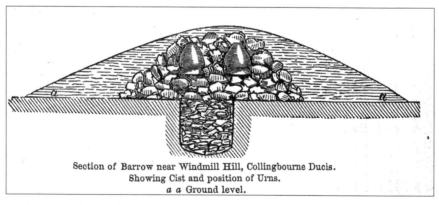

Section of Barrow near Windmill Hill, Collingbourne Ducis.
Showing Cist and position of Urns.
*a a* Ground level.

Lukis produced several sections across the mounds he opened, including this one of a Wiltshire tumulus, showing both the finds and the constructional materials

Lukis's last clerical post was at Wath in Yorkshire, where he dug with Greenwell. His grave in Wath churchyard is marked by this simple cross.

He also wrote works on prehistoric monuments in Brittany, which he had surveyed with his friend Sir Henry Dryden, and Denmark, and was also an expert on church bells and church plate.

In several articles Lukis launched criticisms on the extensive barrow-diggings of Hoare and Cunnington, although the advantage of time and hindsight render these somewhat unfair. Elected FSA in 1855, he died at Wath in December 1892 and is buried in the churchyard.

# MEREWETHER, John (1797–1850).

John Merewether (1797–1850), contentious cleric whose lack of ecclesiastical advancement was an enduring sore point with him. He is best known for his blitzing of over thirty Wiltshire barrows inside one month in 1849.

A somewhat contentious churchman when Dean of Hereford, John Merewether is recorded as being born at Marshfield, Gloucestershire in 1797, though he dedicated his book *Diary of a Dean,* on his 1849 Wiltshire archaeological sojourn 'as a legacy to his native County, whose antiquities he began in early life to study, and never ceased to estimate as of the highest National importance.' He seems to have been interested in tumular activities early in life, and reminisced on his earliest lessons in practical excavation in company with Sir Richard Hoare, which resulted in a turgid poem on the subject, written at the youthful age of seventeen!

Merewether was educated at Oxford and was ordained in 1819. He served in several curacies and attracted the attention of the Duke of Clarence, later William IV. He was chaplain to the Duchess of Clarence, later Queen Adelaide and in 1832 became Dean of Hereford; the king appointed him a deputy clerk of the closet and is said to have asked Lord Melbourne, the Prime Minister, to appoint him to the first available bishopric.

The dean however became increasingly bitter as episcopal vacancies occurred and he was consistently passed over in favour of political appointees. The death of William IV seems to have ended his hopes for advancement, and so soured him that when the Revd Dickson Hampden was proposed Bishop of Hereford in 1847 Merewether strenuously opposed his selection and refused to affix the seal of the Dean and Chapter to the official document recording

Silbury Hill, as depicted by William Stukeley, was one of the targets of Merewether's 1849 delvers, who opened a tunnel into the monument's south side.

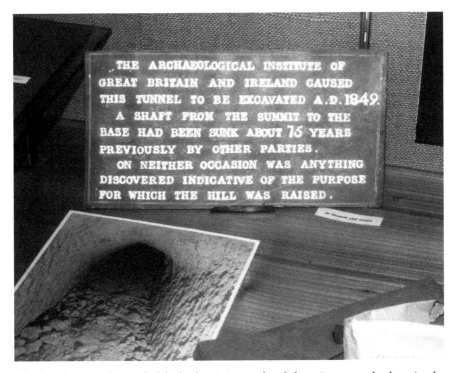

THE ARCHAEOLOGICAL INSTITUTE OF GREAT BRITAIN AND IRELAND CAUSED THIS TUNNEL TO BE EXCAVATED A.D. 1849. A SHAFT FROM THE SUMMIT TO THE BASE HAD BEEN SUNK ABOUT 75 YEARS PREVIOUSLY BY OTHER PARTIES. ON NEITHER OCCASION WAS ANYTHING DISCOVERED INDICATIVE OF THE PURPOSE FOR WHICH THE HILL WAS RAISED.

The lengthy tunnel revealed little, but Merewether left a time capsule deep in the mound, which included this lead sheet containing details of the dig. A photograph of the tunnel can be seen at bottom left.

*Diary of a Dean,* Merewether's account of the 1849 campaign, contains some images, including these illustrations of a barrow circled by a stone kerb and a cremation urn surrounded by a stone cist.

Hampden's formal election. A fruitless letter to the Queen was followed by another to the Prime Minister, Russell, indicating his intention of voting against the bishop elect at the Chapter meeting. Russell's laconic reply commenced with the sentence 'Sir, I had the honour to receive your letter . . . in which you intimate to me your intention of violating the law.' The dean even questioned the legality of the election and refused to attend the enthronement.

Merewether was an enthusiastic antiquary who was elected FSA in 1836 and took a great interest in the restoration of Hereford Cathedral. Archaeologically speaking he has become notorious for the whirlwind blitzing of some thirty-one tumuli on the Wiltshire Downs in the summer of 1849. The dean was an early supporter of the BAA, becoming a vice president on its formation in 1843. When a schism developed within the BAA hierarchy he defected to the seceding Archaeological Institute and organised an excavation programme during the Institute's 1849 congress at Salisbury.

Within twenty-eight days in July/August Merewether directed the excoriation of some thirty-one tumuli, plus the driving of a 264 foot long tunnel into Silbury Hill from the south under the direction of a railway engineer. A great archaeological enthusiast, Merewether's delight in his Wiltshire expedition shines through in his readable 1851 description, *Diary of a Dean,* published after his death. Though the barrow-openings were fairly execrable, drawings of burials, gravegoods and plans of tumuli do at least rescue some details from his meagre accounts.

Merewether has become notorious for his wholesale assault during that long-ago summer, but he was at least sufficiently committed to record his researches. He died in April 1850 and was interred in the Lady Chapel of his beloved cathedral. Five lancet windows were later fitted with stained glass to his memory.

# MITCHELL, Samuel (1803–1868).

Samuel Mitchell (1803–68), Sheffield
solicitor and minor digger, worked with
both William and Thomas Bateman, and
dug his first tumulus at the tender age
of fifteen!

A minor figure in antiquarian circles, though worth recording as the link
between the Batemans, father and son, Mitchell was born in Sheffield in 1803,
son of a merchant, and followed in his father's business, later travelling widely
in Norway, Russia and Europe. Referred to as 'a young and zealous antiquary'
his first barrow-dig, if the dating is reliable, took place in Derbyshire in
1818, when he was a stripling of sixteen! He wrote accounts of his barrow-
openings in his *Memoranda,* now in the British Library, and much of his early
explorations were in the company of William Bateman (1787–1835), country
gentleman and collector, and father of the more famous Thomas.

Bateman and Mitchell carried out several short barrow-digging campaigns
in 1825-26 in and around the former's Youlgrave home in Derbyshire, and the
latter also dug several cairns on the North Derbyshire moors at the same time.
'Pressing business obligations' kept Mitchell from any further archaeological
activity until the 1830s when he opened an unspecified number of cairns
around Leam and Bamford, finding as he recorded nothing other 'than urns
and burnt bones.' He assisted Thomas Bateman in the reinvestigation of the
Gib Hill cairn, the largest barrow in Derbyshire, in 1848, and was operating on
the Derbyshire moors as late as 1850 when he probed ten mounds on Ramsley
Moor, with little success. Mitchell obviously dug into many tumuli but his
only excavation reports were descriptions of those he dug with Thomas's

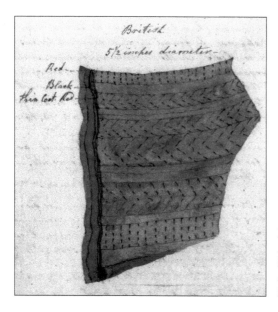

Mitchell's unpublished *Memoranda* contains some images, including this sketch of an obvious beaker sherd found in a Derbyshire cairn in 1818.

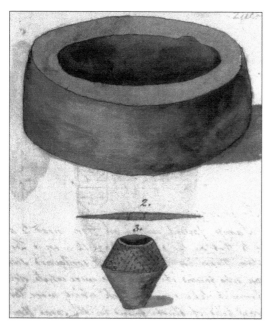

Mitchell's drawings of an urn, miniature cup and bronze awl found by William Bateman and himself in the Lark's Low cairn in Derbyshire. Mitchell firmly believed that most of the barrows he dug with Bateman covered 'Roman' interments.

father, where he gave valuable accounts of the structures and materials of the barrows, though he was inclined to attribute most of them, incorrectly, to the Romano-British era.

Mitchell was a long-term member of the Sheffield Literary and Philosophical Society, and was elected president in 1856. He died in September 1868 in his native city, his *Memoranda* his enduring memorial.

# MILES, William Augustus (1796–1851).

The Deverel Barrow, Dorset, excavated by William Augustus Miles (1786–1851) in 1825 and the subject of his famous book published the following year.

William Miles, author of the interesting and instructive little work *The Deverel Barrow* (1826) led a life hidden in obscurity. Though ostensibly the eldest offspring of William Augustus Miles Senior (1753–1817), political writer, he may have been the illegitimate son of William IV who certainly supported his application for the post of secretary of the Colonisation Committee for South Australia in 1835.

Born in 1798, Miles trained for service with the East India Company at Haileybury School, but was expelled and disowned by his brothers after his father's death. He later held a number of civil appointments in England before moving to New South Wales in 1840 as Commissioner of Police in Sydney. He had worked in the Privy Council office, as assistant commissioner of inquiry into the Poor Law, as assistant to the commission of inquiry into the state of hand-loom weavers, and as a commissioner of public charities. What he was doing in rural Dorset in 1825 is anyone's guess, but his little literary curiosity shows he was no stranger either to the county or barrow-digging 'having at various times' opened a number.

Miles's illustration shows the centre of the barrow which covered an extensive series of urn cremations which gave their name to the Deverel-Rimbury pottery series.

This fine depiction has the Shapwick Barrow, Sturminster Marshall, as its subject. It was opened in 1838 and was the centrepiece of the Revd Charles Woolls's little book, *The Barrow Diggers*, published the following year.

Published in 1826, *The Deverel Barrow* describes the opening of the tumulus which gives its name to the book. It was investigated a year earlier in November, revealing a whole series of urns of various types which were later classified as examples of the Deverel-Rimbury series. For its time the excavation was noteworthy for Miles's care with the vessels, some of which were damp and required great care in their removal. Many of the pots were illustrated, and a view of the mound interior was also provided. The introduction to the book was somewhat florid and imaginative, but the description of the dig was objective and factual, with the writer 'confining myself to narrative, not indulging in conjecture.' One purple passage in the work is of high literary merit, describing as it does an evening spent on the bleak Dorset down as the digging party lit fires to dry out some of the urns *in situ,* the author painting a fine word picture of the nocturnal scene.

Little else is known of Miles's archaeological activities. He came into contact with the Metropolitan Police in 1834 and was assistant commissioner to the Royal Commission on rural constabulary between 1836–39. The Prime Minister, Russell, recommended him for the post of Commissioner of the Sydney Police Force, a post he held, not without contention, until enforced retirement in 1850.

Whilst in Sydney Miles became interested in Aboriginal rock art and wrote an appendix to George Agnan's 1847 book on the subject. He was also a corresponding member of the Ethnological Society of London. He died in Sydney in April 1851 at the early age of 55, remembered for his one minor antiquarian curiosity.

The other 'unpretending little work' worth mentioning is *The Barrow Diggers,* published anonymously by the Revd Charles Woolls in 1839. It marked the 'exceedingly agreeable' opening of the Shapwick Barrow the previous year, the text imitating the dialogue between Hamlet and the gravedigger in Shakespeare's tragedy. The book's importance lies in the explanatory notes which contain useful information regarding Dorset antiquities.

Charles Woolls is an elusive character of whom little is known. He graduated from Pembroke College, Oxford in 1828 and in 1838 held the living of Sturminster Marshall in which parish the large mound was situated. The famous plate showing the excoriation of the barrow appears in his charming little book.

# MORTIMER, John Robert (1825–1911).

John Robert Mortimer (1825–1911), east Yorkshire farmer, who dedicated his life to exploring the burial mounds clustered on his native wolds, and who erected a purpose-built museum to house his vast collection.

John Mortimer, last of the great English barrow-diggers, was born in Fimber, in the Yorkshire East Riding, in June 1825, son of a wolds farmer. He began a successful corn merchant's business which he relocated to Driffield in 1869 and where he lived for the rest of his life. His scientific interests were kindled by a visit to the Great Exhibition of 1851 and he began collecting fossils and flints from the wolds, encouraging farm workers to bring him these casually found 'Mortimers.'

Mortimer began exploring Yorkshire barrows in 1863, often with the help of his younger brother Robert and an appropriate labour force. By the end of his life he had opened 304, plus 70 in the Iron Age 'Danes' Graves' cemetery near Driffield, some of the latter in association with William Greenwell; he had mended fences with the canon after earlier spats connected with the cleric's mode of barrow-opening. He had also mapped the linear earthworks crossing the southern wolds, and investigated several Anglian cemeteries. His methodology was in advance of the times, with large sections of tumuli opened up and stratigraphical relationships noted. Structures in and under burial mounds were interpreted and barrow construction and composition described. Soil samples and human remains were analysed, plaster casts made of postholes, and finds securely provenanced to site level and context.

Mortimer's major work was *Forty Years' Researches in British and Saxon Burial Mounds of East Yorkshire,* published in 1905. The book mapped the sites of fifteen barrow groups he had worked on, including plans of the cemeteries and individual tumuli, showing the interments and other features. The finds were illustrated from superb drawings by his youngest daughter Agnes, then aged between thirteen and nineteen years old.

The burgeoning collection was moved to a purpose-built museum in Driffield in 1878, equipped with display galleries and workshops. Sadly, his business, whose profits had largely funded his diggings, went bankrupt in 1887 at a time of severe agricultural depression, and from that date his operations had to be financed by others. Keen to ensure that the assemblage remained in Yorkshire, Mortimer offered it to East Riding County Council at half its value. After much vacillation, Colonel G. H. Clarke purchased it and it moved to Hull Museum in 1914.

Fully self-taught, Mortimer confined his operations strictly to the region where he lived. His collection, together with those of Hoare, Bateman and Greenwell provide the foundations on which subsequent work on British prehistory has been built. He died in Driffield in August 1911; 'his fine, tall figure' wrote his obituarist 'will be greatly missed.'

A rare photograph of a Mortimer barrow-dig, this illustration shows Riggs 183 under excavation in June 1875, looking west.

A-digging we will go! Mortimer holds the reins as his opening party pose for posterity in their horse-drawn transport some time in the 1860s. His brother Robert sits back-to-back with him, whilst behind Robert is John's long-term foreman, Thomas Hebb.

The vast size of the Duggleby Howe barrow, and indeed the excavation section, is apparent in this photograph of the dig, taken in 1890. Mortimer is the central figure on the left, with site foreman Thomas Hebb at centre foreground. The youth at centre right may be Thomas Sheppard, later curator of Hull Museum.

A significant photograph showing Greenwell, on the right clutching a human femur, and Mortimer, centre, posing in one of the Danes' Graves Iron Age barrows, one of sixty opened by the pair in 1898. On the left is a mutual friend Thomas Boynton.

# PEGGE, Samuel (1704–1796).

Samuel Pegge (1704–96), cleric, polymath, writer on a variety of subjects, and one of the earliest authorities to study the prehistoric sites of his native Derbyshire.

Samuel Pegge was born in Chesterfield, Derbyshire in November 1704, son of a merchant. He was a polymath of wide learning who was educated at Cambridge and took holy orders in 1730. His earliest livings were in Kent where he first developed his antiquarian interests, collecting coins and books and researching and writing on various subjects. He returned to Chesterfield in 1746 as vicar of Brampton, but the parishioners opposed his induction and he went back to Kent; it was not until 1751 that he was appointed rector of Whittington church, a living he held until his death.

Pegge was elected FSA in 1751 and for the next four decades produced a wealth of antiquarian writings to its journal, *Archaeologia* and other publications such as the *Gentleman's Magazine*. His output was prolific and diverse, but he was particularly interested in the early history of his native county. This interest resulted in papers on the 'Druidical remains in the Peak' the opening of a tumulus in Derbyshire, and a 'Disquisition on the Lows and Barrows of the Peak' followed by 'Some observations on the Stanton Moor urns' – prehistoric pots dug up by his great friend and fellow antiquary, Major Hayman Rooke (1723–1806) of Mansfield Woodhouse, who opened a

Perhaps the earliest drawings of prehistoric pottery and gravegoods ever published, this woodcut accompanied Pegge's dissertation on artefacts found by his friend Hayman Rooke in a cairn on Stanton Moor in 1784. The pendant at bottom right is either shale or jet.

A contemporary painting of escutcheons from a bronze hanging bowl found at Garratt Low, Derbyshire, and once in Pegge's possession.

number of cairns in Derbyshire and a Roman villa near his Nottinghamshire home. The urns were illustrated in the *Archaeologia,* and must represent the earliest drawings of prehistoric vessels ever published in Britain.

Archaeologically speaking, Pegge was a theorist, and it is doubtful if he ever sank a spade into a barrow or earthwork unlike his more practical friend Rooke. His collections included a number of ancient artefacts, including the enamelled escutcheons from an Anglian hanging bowl which accompanied a burial found in a tumulus near Youlgrave. Pegge was also interested in the later history of the county, and contributed articles on the Roman roads of the region, and the history of Bolsover and Peak castles. He also published the inscriptions on Roman lead pigs found in Derbyshire, and gathered numerous relics from various periods of time.

Pegge's many publications on a variety of topics resulted in the award of an LL.D by the University of Oxford in 1791. He recalled that the great German composer Haydn received a doctorate 'along with me.' Though sometimes derided by later scholars, Pegge not only collated historical data amassed by earlier antiquaries but added his own contribution to numismatics and local prehistoric and Roman studies. His pioneering work pointed contemporary students to the value of topographical research, writing and publishing, laying the foundations for later local historians to build upon.

Dr Pegge died in February 1796 and was buried in his local church. Unfortunately his memorial tablet was destroyed by fire over a century later.

# PENGELLY, William (1812–1894).

William Pengelly (1812–94), once described as 'of good presence and benevolent expression' is best remembered as a cave-explorer in his native Devon, whose careful excavations revealed the true antiquity of the deposits he unearthed.

Described as a small man 'of good presence and benevolent expression of face' William Pengelly was born in 1812 at East Looe, Cornwall, son of a sea captain. He spent four years working on his father's coasting vessel from the age of twelve, before embarking on a course of self-education after which he opened a school in Torquay in 1836. He became a private tutor ten years later and, noted as a lucid and attractive speaker, began a long career lecturing up and down the country on the antiquity of early man. His desire to educate the masses led him to found the Torquay Young Men's Society in 1837 (renamed the Mechanics' Institute in 1846), the Torquay Natural History Society in 1844 and the Devonshire Association for the Advancement of Literature, Science and Art in 1862.

Pengelly's early interests focused on the geology and palaeontology of Devon and human prehistory, and his research led to his election as FRS in 1863. However his most lasting contribution to science related to his investigation of the Devon caves and their prehistory. Kent's Cavern, in Torquay, had been excavated in the 1820s by the Revd John MacEnery who had unearthed stone tools in association with extinct animal bones. In 1846 Pengelly was asked to continue researches at the site, but cave exploration was in its infancy and he disagreed with colleagues over the interpretation of the finds.

In 1858 the quarrying of a rockface overlooking Brixham harbour revealed a series of fissures in the limestone, and the Geological Society formed an investigation committee, appointing Pengelly to supervise the operations. He used an improved three-dimensional method of excavation and recording,

First revealed by quarrying in 1858 Brixham Cave was excavated by Pengelly and as this contemporary poster proclaims, subsequently became a visitor attraction.

This early photograph of Kent's Cavern, thoroughly investigated by Pengelly, shows site foreman William Smerdon posed at the narrow entrance to the site.

Pengelly's advanced three-dimensional system of cave excavation is clearly shown in this diagrammatic exposition of his archaeological method.

unearthing considerable numbers of flint tools associated with the bones of extinct fauna in the cave earth. Pengelly later reported that the scientific world had said his statements on the finds were impossible. He retorted 'we had not said they were possible, only that they were true.'

In 1865 Pengelly returned to Kent's Cavern with the support of the British Association for the Advancement of Science. He worked at the cave until 1880, further refining his techniques and providing unmistakable proof that the early denizens of Devon were contemporaries of the mammoth and woolly rhinoceros. A man of great energy, charming, genial and with a ready wit, he received many honours during his later life. Pengelly died in Torquay in March 1894 and a Memorial Hall, erected by public subscription to his memory, was subsequently built onto the Museum of the Natural History Society in the town itself.

# PITT RIVERS, Augustus Henry Lane Fox (1827–1900).

Augustus Henry Lane Fox Pitt Rivers (1827–1900), father of modern archaeological methods, was famous for his innovations and a series of careful explorations on his Cranborne estate.

Pitt Rivers was born at Hope Hall, Bramham, Yorkshire in April 1827, son of an army officer. He assumed the name Pitt Rivers in 1880 on inheriting the estates of his cousin Horace Pitt, sixth Baron Rivers, an extremely wealthy man. He was educated at Sandhurst and commissioned into the Grenadier Guards in 1845. In 1851 he was seconded to the commission on the adoption of the rifle into the army, and his first collection was an assemblage of historic firearms. In 1854 he served in the Crimea and was present at the bloody battle of the Alma, followed by further service in Malta, Canada and Ireland.

Pitt Rivers's firearms collection gradually expanded to include a mass of ethnographic material which he used to explain his theory on the evolution of culture. This theory embodied the idea of typology, the realisation that objects could be placed in a chronological sequence, a crucial concept for archaeology. The collections were given to Oxford University where they form the basis of the Pitt Rivers Museum, opened in 1884.

Pitt Rivers's interest in field archaeology dated from his time in Ireland where he surveyed a number of prehistoric forts. He was elected FSA in 1864 and three years later was assisting Canon Greenwell in barrow-digging on the Yorkshire Wolds. He recalled 'my first lessons as an excavator were derived from Canon Greenwell in the course of which I obtained a large amount of

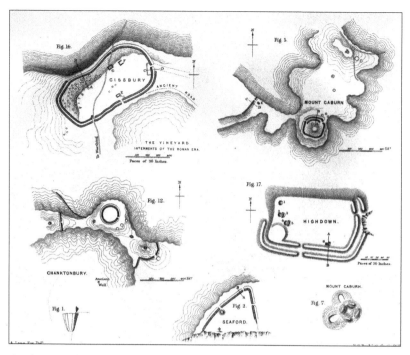

A selection of plans of Sussex hillforts, drawn with Pitt Rivers's usual military precision, and published in 1868.

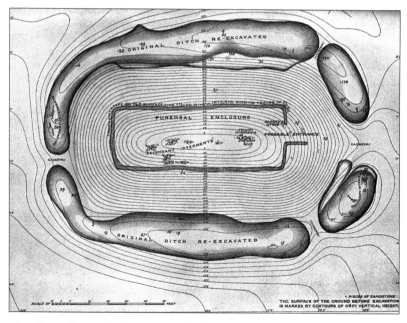

The General's meticulous plan of the Wor Barrow and its ditches was outstanding for its time. The whole site was completely excavated in 1894 in a thoroughly exemplary operation.

The final stages of the Wor Barrow dig, with the chalk pillars acting as markers relating to the mound's original height and stratification. Note the large-scale area excavation to the right, and the General's carriage in the middle distance.

An example of the bronze discs left by Pitt Rivers in the sites he excavated, with the date clearly stamped.

useful information that has been a constant source of enjoyment and interest to me.' Pitt Rivers surveyed and excavated flint mines and hill forts in Sussex and discovered stone tools and extinct animal bones in the drift gravels of the Thames Valley. In 1876 he was elected FRS and in 1882 became the first Inspector of Ancient Monuments, travelling throughout Britain, inspecting sites and making recommendations for scheduling. He retired from the army in the 1870s, retaining the rank of lieutenant general.

However, Pitt Rivers's real life's work began in 1880 when he inherited the vast Cranborne Chase estate in Dorset and Wiltshire, where he spent the last twenty years of his life excavating a whole series of earthworks, ranging from the Neolithic to the Romano-British and Dark Age periods. Total excavation with full publication was his credo, and a range of sites were tackled in a series of military-style campaigns led by supervisors and draughtsmen using large labour gangs. The operations included the scientific dismantling of the Neolithic Wor Barrow, a series of Roman settlements, and Dark Age defensive banks such as Wansdyke and Bokerly Dike as well as some thirty tumuli scattered across his property which were totally removed and rebuilt.

The operations were lavishly published in four privately-printed volumes, *Excavations in Cranborne Chase,* which appeared between 1887 and 1898. The books describe his investigations fully, and the text is augmented with numerous illustrations, measured plans and sections, relic tables, descriptions of crania and a thorough analysis of animal bones. All the finds were displayed in a museum at Farnham in Dorset.

From the few clues we have, Pitt Rivers was not an especially likeable personality, but a moody, querulous individual with little humour. Nevertheless he transformed antiquarianism into archaeology, insisting on contextual recording and precisely plotting the position of every find, including the most mundane sherd of pottery. One of the finest excavators of his time, his precision in publishing information in plan and section drawings at least rivals modern practice.

Considered the true founder of British archaeology for his innovations and carefully recorded operations, Pitt Rivers died in May 1900 at his Cranborne Chase home, Rushmore, and, to the end a disciple of modernism, was cremated at Woking. His ashes were interred in Tollard Royal Church.

# ROLLESTON, George (1829–1881).

George Rolleston (1829–81), child prodigy, anatomist, craniologist and barrow-opener, who worked with Canon Greenwell, principally on the Cotswold long barrows.

Described as 'richly endowed, but diffuse' – presumably relating to his intellect – George Rolleston was born at Maltby Hall, Rotherham, Yorkshire, in July 1829, son of the local vicar and squire. A child prodigy, he won a scholarship to Oxford where he obtained a first class degree in classics in 1850. He determined to study medicine and qualified MD four years later. In 1855 he served as a physician at the military hospital in Smyrna in the closing stages of the Crimean War, touring Palestine before his return home.

Tall and broad shouldered, and a man of considerable charm, Rolleston returned to Oxford as physician to the Radcliffe Infirmary and reader in anatomy, and in 1860 was chosen as first Linacre professor of anatomy. Rolleston's great learning and formidable energy resulted in a department which taught a range of allied subjects including comparative anatomy and archaeology. He was here associated with the introduction of the teaching of human sciences and helped shape the way they were presented in a wider context.

Rolleston attended the meeting of the British Association at Oxford when Darwin's recently published *Origin of Species* was debated, and came away impressed with Darwinism. He began studying brain development and skull classification, and amassed a collection of crania which was eventually presented to Oxford University Museum.

In 1857 Rolleston obtained his MD and was elected FRCP in 1859 and FRS three years later. He played a prominent part in the public and academic life of Oxford between 1850 and 1881, including helping to promote the

'Alas, poor Yorick!' An amusing cartoon entitled 'The Modern Resurrection Man' showing Rolleston's penchant for barrow-digging and craniology.

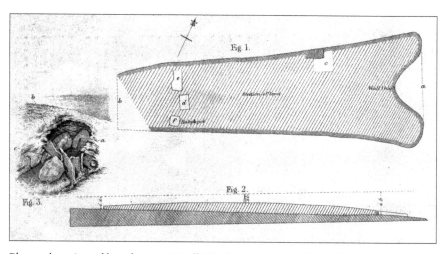

Plan and section of long barrow 'Swell VI' plus a drawing of the chamber and passage found in 'Swell VII', both in Gloucestershire, and both investigated by Rolleston.

provision of mains drainage and the isolation of smallpox victims during the 1871 epidemic. What little leisure he had was devoted to the exploration of archaeological sites, particularly the Cotswold long barrows of which he opened a number, often in association with Canon Greenwell and the Revd David Royce, vicar of Nether Swell. Here his interest was in the physical anatomy of the burials, though his monograph *On the People of the Long Barrow Period* (1876) included plans and sections of three sites he examined.

Rolleston also dug at an Anglo-Saxon cemetery at Frilford in Berkshire and at sundry other burial sites. He provided the section on crania in Canon Greenwell's 1877 *British Barrows*, analysing the skulls and presenting conclusions concerning their ethnic origins. He was also a close friend of another archaeologist, Pitt Rivers. Failing health, probably the result of pressure of work, led him to winter in 1880–1881 on the French Riviera, but he died the following June at his Oxford home at the early age of 51. He was buried in the Holywell Cemetery in the city.

# SALT, Micah (1847–1915).

Micah Salt (1847–1915), Buxton tailor and outfitter, and self-taught archaeologist who may have been a natural son of Sir John Harpur Crewe.

Micah Salt was born in 1848 at Hollinsclough, Staffordshire, on the very border of  Derbyshire, quite possibly the illegitimate progeny of Sir John Harpur Crewe of Calke Abbey. His mother, Eliza Salt, was unmarried and lived with her parents. She bore two other sons, Micah being the youngest of the three. Sir John paid for the boys' education in the village, and Micah later named his youngest son Vauncey, the same name as Sir John's eldest boy.

As a young boy Micah watched a digging party opening a cairn on Hollinsclough Moor in 1862; impelled by curiosity he deepened the opening after the explorers had gone, and discovered a cremation with a bronze brooch. Years afterwards he found out that the men he had observed were led by Llewellynn Jewitt and John Lucas.

Micah Salt worked as a silk-weaver in Macclesfield before moving to Buxton in 1866, eventually setting up in business as a tailor and outfitter. As well as an archaeologist he was an ornithologist and a collector, especially of paintings, engravings and old Staffordshire china. Described rather patronisingly as 'an intelligent tradesman' Salt began his explorations by digging at caves and rock shelters around his adopted town, finding much evidence of Romano-British occupation. He was a self-taught practitioner who learned by his own experience, with a labour force provided by 'the assistance cheerfully given by his sons.'

Deepdale Cave, south of Buxton, where Salt found evidence of human and animal occupation as far apart as the Palaeolithic and Romano-British eras.

Salt's archaeological finds are divided between the Poole's Cavern show cave display, seen here, and nearby Buxton Museum.

Salt's grave, in Buxton's municipal cemetery, is marked with this superb copy of the Anglian cross in Eyam churchyard, Derbyshire.

Salt also dug at some dozen round cairns, most of them recorded by his friend William Turner who recorded the former's activities in his 1899 work *Ancient Remains near Buxton – the Archaeological Explorations of Micah Salt*. Among the tumuli opened was the prominent example at Grin Low, overlooking Buxton, and the chambered cairn at Fivewells. Salt's work had some system, guided as it was by his mentor, John Ward, an enlightened archaeologist often present at the excavations. Ward wrote up most of Salt's digs, drew the plans, sections and gravegoods from the latter's notes, and doubtless provided the precise descriptions in Turner's book. Micah Salt died in 1915, and was buried in Buxton cemetery, his grave marked by a fine copy of the Anglian stone cross in Eyam churchyard.

# SKINNER, John (1772–1839).

John Skinner (1772–1839), Somerset rector, antiquary, etymologist and barrow-digger, who ultimately found himself at war with his children, his parishioners and the world at large.

John Skinner, born at Claverton near Bath in 1772, emerges as one of the more tragic figures in the story of Nineteenth century antiquarianism. He was educated at Oxford  and entered Lincoln's Inn in 1794 but then decided to take holy orders. By this time he was keeping journals of his travels, and after various curacies his uncle purchased the living of Camerton in his native Somerset, which he held until his death.

Skinner's life at Camerton was soon blighted by a number of family deaths between 1810 and 1812, including his eldest brother, a naval officer, and his two sisters, followed by his youngest daughter and his wife Anna. In 1820 his eldest daughter also died young. 'Tormented and querulous, at the same time consistent and able' Skinner found his rural parish no easy ride, and battled continuously with everyone in sight, a battle vividly recalled in his diary and journals. His one respite was antiquarianism, and as well as pursuing the belief that his village was the site of Tacitus's Camulodunum, and studying etymology, he indulged in the pursuit of barrow-digging, mainly into sites around his own parish.

In the second decade of the Nineteenth century the cleric opened some twenty-six tumuli, mainly in execrable style, often using unsupervised workmen. His painfully crude work included the examination of six barrows in one afternoon, lamenting that his men 'missed the centre, or did not dig deep enough.' On another occasion four mounds produced no results, as his labourers 'digged wide of the cists as he was not on the spot to direct them, and could not rectify his mistake except by working the ground all over

Three of the Priddy Nine barrows, seen here, were just a few of the many tumuli he dug into, rather badly, during his tenure at Camerton.

Skinner's most important work was at the Stoney Littleton long barrow, which he explored on behalf of Sir Richard Hoare, and did his utmost to protect against the depredations of local vandals.

Despite committing suicide, Skinner was interred in Camerton churchyard where the graves of many of his family can still be seen.

again.' Perhaps his most important task was the clearing and preservation of the Stoney Littleton chambered long barrow which he undertook at the behest of his friend, Sir Richard Hoare. As was common for the time few of the sites were precisely located, except well-known groups such as the Priddy Nine barrows, and the gravegoods culled from the tumuli have not survived.

Skinner was scrupulous in his pastoral duties, hardworking but humourless, and quick with sententious advice. Sadly he and his surviving children shared little empathy, frequently quarrelling violently. His two sons were slow in finding careers, and the eldest boy died in 1833 of tuberculosis, another blow to Skinner's faltering sanity, compounded by the death of his surviving brother the year previously. His mental health began a steady decline and by 1839 he was seriously troubled. One October night in that year he made his way to the beech wood behind his rectory and blew out his brains with his pistol.

Skinner's will bequeathed some 146 volumes of manuscripts to the British Library, including diaries, tours and antiquarian items, and since his death he has emerged as a significant diarist. Twenty-five further volumes of his papers were discovered in 1933 and selected parts of his journal have been published. Bleak though his diaries appear, Skinner sadly failed to empathise with his admittedly difficult parishioners, but his writings are moving and significant documents in the picture of an early Nineteenth century rural English parish.

# STUKELEY, William (1687–1765).

William Stukeley (1687–1765), doctor, cleric, first of the great English field archaeologists and a barrow-digging pioneer.

William Stukeley was born in November 1687 at Holbeach, Lincolnshire, the son of an attorney. First apprenticed as a clerk in his father's law firm, he became a student of medicine at Cambridge in 1703. Stukeley graduated as a bachelor of medicine and moved to Boston in 1710 where he practised as a physician. Seven years later he removed to London and in 1718 became a member of the re-established Society of Antiquaries, being appointed the body's first secretary. In 1719 he took the degree of MD at Cambridge and was admitted a fellow of the Royal College of Physicians.

Between 1719 and 1743 Stukeley undertook a series of regular campaigns which led to the amassing of a vast collection of material dealing with native prehistoric antiquities. He set out to 'oblige the curious in the Antiquitys of Britain' by compiling 'an account of places and things from inspection, not compiled from others' labours, or travels in one's study.' The result was his *Itinerarium Curiosum* of 1724 which detailed, with numerous engravings, a host of field monuments and other objects of antiquarian interest. The work embodied the suggestion that certain monuments predated the Roman period, and that continental incursions could have at least partly shaped Britain's past.

Stukeley illustrated many of his works; in this view the Roman road the Ackling Dyke, in Dorset, cuts through a Bronze Age disc barrow in the Oakley Down group, proving that the barrow preceded the road.

*The Cove of the Northern temple.*

Stukeley haunted both Stonehenge and Avebury, producing invaluable information and views of both circles. This woodcut shows the great cove at 'Abury' as he saw it in the 1720s.

This panorama shows the now-destroyed Sanctuary stone circle which stood at the end of the Kennet Avenue which ran south-east from Avebury. The West Kennet long barrow can be seen at centre left, with Silbury Hill visible further to the right.

Among his excursions, Stukeley traversed Hadrian's Wall, and witnessed the destruction of the sarsens at Avebury, of which he drew a lively 'groundplot' in 1724. A frequent visitor to Stonehenge, the doctor assigned both vast structures' origins to druidism – 'the aboriginal patriarchal religion.' So fiercely did he promote his beliefs that his intimates were wont to refer to him as 'the arch-druid of the age.' In fact by the end of Stukeley's life more or less everything began and ended with the druids.

The doctor was also one of the first antiquaries to dig purposefully for knowledge, opening a number of burial mounds, mainly on Salisbury Plain, leaving coins and tokens as a means of recording his presence. He noted the structures of tumuli, and described their contents objectively if sometimes over-imaginatively, classifying the mound shapes in a series of peculiar and fanciful labels including 'King' barrows, 'Archdruid' barrows and 'Priestess's' barrows. The 'learned doctor' however, later described as 'a strange compound of simplicity, drollery, absurdity, ingenuity, superstition and antiquarianism,' merits attention for his pioneer fieldwork on Stonehenge and Avebury, carried out during the summers of 1718 to 1724.

At the former monument, which he regarded as 'one of the noblest antiquities now left upon earth' Stukeley discovered the earthwork avenue and the nearby cursus, correctly identified the stones' astronomical alignment and coined the word 'trilithon.' At Avebury he vividly chronicled the destruction of the great sarsen orthostats, and traced out the Kennet stone avenue and the all-but-vanished Beckhampton avenue. His researches bore fruit in two great monographs, *Stonehenge: a Temple Restor'd to the British Druids* (1740) and *Abury: a Temple of the British Druids* (1743). The works have great value as descriptions of both sites as they appeared at the time, though their merit is obscured by Stukeley's weird prognostications and his insistence on relating their shape and form to suit his fantasies.

Stukeley moved to Grantham in 1726 and three years later took holy orders, obtaining the living of Stamford in 1730 where he founded a literary and antiquarian society. In 1747 he moved back to London where he died in February 1765 after suffering a stroke. Stukeley was a polymath, with manifold interests, and was considered by his contemporaries as somewhat of an eccentric with an unfettered imagination. In truth, his dedication, sharp eye and undiminished enthusiasm mark him out as the true father of British field archaeology.

# THURNAM, John (1810–1873).

John Thurnam (1810–73), doctor, craniologist and prolific barrow-digger both in his native Yorkshire and later in Wessex.

John Thurnam was born in December 1810 at Lingcroft, near York, son of a manufacturer. He studied for the medical profession, becoming a member of the RCS in 1834 and graduating MD in 1846. He was subsequently elected FRCP in 1859. Thurnam served at Westminster Hospital from 1834–1838 before his appointment as medical superintendent of the Friends' Retreat at York where he committed himself to the study of archaeology and crania. He supervised his first barrow-digs on the Yorkshire Wolds at Acklam in 1849 on behalf of the Yorkshire Antiquarian and Philosophical Society, though the work was rather uncritical, one observer referring to the digging party as 'that pack of asses, Thurnam and Co.'

Thurnam's real work commenced in 1849 when he was appointed medical superintendent of the Wiltshire County Asylum, then being built at Devizes. He moved to Wiltshire in 1851, one unkind critic noting that the 'coxcomb puppy' had 'departed to join his relatives at the Wilts. Asylum.' At the same time he married, and a gentler observer later felt that 'if marriage improves me as much as it has done him, I shall have just cause to be thankful.' In the 1850s

Thurnam dug at the West Kennet long barrow in 1859, producing this image of the central passage. Inexplicably he failed to note pairs of side chambers masked by blocking stones, leading to a misinterpretation of the type of site the barrow represented.

Among the many long barrows visited by Thurnam was Belas Knap in Gloucestershire. This illustration reveals the fine blind entrance set in its horned forecourt, with visitors hastening to inspect the excavations.

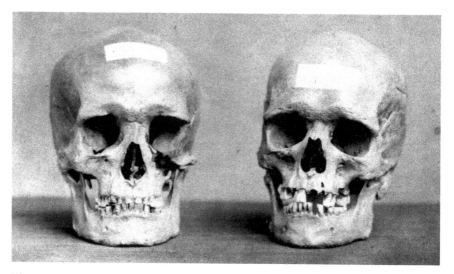

Thurnam was a craniological expert and was much interested in these two skulls from Belas Knap as they exemplified both the long-headed and round-headed racial types, though the latter was almost certainly a subsequent deposit.

Thurnam collaborated with Dr Joseph Barnard Davis in the publication of *Crania Britannica,* a mammoth study of ancient British skulls.

During his lifetime Thurnam excavated nearly one hundred long and round barrows, mainly in Wessex, plus a few outliers on the Cotswolds. One preoccupation was to recover skulls and other bones for comparative purposes and to further his own researches. One rich source of supply were the tumuli opened by William Cunnington, who recorded inhumations but invariably left them *in situ.* Thurnam reopened many of these mounds simply for the bones they contained. Long barrows, particularly the chambered variety, were of great interest to him, including famous examples such as West Kennett, Belas Knap and Hetty Pegler's Tump; here again he sought the clusters of inhumed bones huddled in the stone vaults. Few observations on structure, size and materials ever appeared in print. After his death his collection of crania were passed to Cambridge University and the barrow gravegoods to the British Museum.

Thurnam's labours on burial mounds doubtless led him to complete his classic syntheses on long and round barrows embodied in a two-part monograph *On Ancient British Barrows, especially on those of Wiltshire and the Adjoining Counties,* which appeared in *Archaeologia* 42 (1868) and 43 (1871). He worked hard on these pioneer papers, work pursued part-time and which at least one acquaintance believed led to his premature death. The two extensive reports form the basis of all subsequent barrow interpretation, assessing the evidence from excavations and analysing the mound types and relics. These studies represent Thurnam's real claim to archaeological fame, the collation of two valuable repositories of information on barrows, still of some value today. His work laid the foundations on which subsequent researchers have been able to build.

Described as efficient, zealous, dapper and professional by some colleagues, he was also dismissed as stuffy and long-winded by others. Even his coadjutor, Davis, commented on 'the distance of his personal manners.' Davis also wrote 'His is a peculiar mind. He appears to see nothing but himself in the present, and nothing but himself in the future. I am frequently obliged to oppose an unrelenting firmness, when compliance would be much more gratifying to me.' Thurnam died at Bishop's Cannings, near Devizes in September 1873, a significant pioneer in Nineteenth century archaeological studies.

# WARD, John (1856–1922).

John Ward (1856–1922), museum curator and archaeologist who guided Micah Salt's Derbyshire operations and later dug prehistoric and Roman sites in South Wales.

John Ward was born in Derby in 1856, where he made an early career as a pharmaceutical chemist. However, he developed an interest in archaeology and was active in antiquarian circles in his native town, serving on the council of the Derbyshire Archaeological Society and excavating a few Neolithic and Early Bronze Age burial mounds in the Peak during the 1880s and 1890s, plus the odd cave and occupation site. His operations were distinguished by careful observation and his skills as an artist and draughtsman ensured that the papers he published were well-illustrated with plans, sections and drawings of the finds.

Little is known of Ward's personal life though contemporaries spoke of his scholarship and organising ability, and his possession of 'a kindly courtesy which made him esteemed by all with whom he came in contact.' In the 1890s he met Micah Salt of Buxton, guiding the latter's archaeological bent into scientific channels, helping with his barrow and cave investigations and writing up the accounts of his digs which were later published with appropriate illustrations.

In 1893 Ward was appointed curator of the Cardiff Museum and Art Gallery and elected FSA at the same time. He set out to enlarge and organise the museum collections, and give them a Welsh emphasis. He acquired a series of obsolete articles of domestic and rural life and took casts of early Christian monuments, many of which remain in the galleries of the National Museum of Wales. A capable modeller, he fashioned a series of geological models which won a silver medal at the Paris Exhibition of 1900.

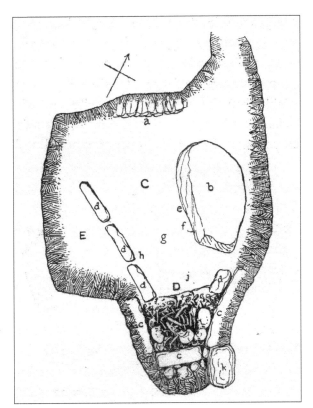

Ward did much of his early work in Derbyshire; he drew this plan of a small chambered cairn he investigated at Harborough Rocks in 1889.

Ward had some expertise as an illustrator, a skill put to good use in his sketch of a chamber in the Fivewells cairn near Taddington in the Peak.

In 1914 Ward excavated the Tinkinswood megalithic tomb in Glamorgan, recovering the bones of some forty individuals and restoring the chamber and forecourt. Note the massive forty ton capstone covering the vault.

Ward maintained his connections with Derbyshire, and wrote the early chapters of the *Victoria History of the County of Derby*, published in 1905. In 1900 the excavation of the Roman fort of Gelligaer in Glamorgan commenced under the *aegis* of the museum and the Cardiff Naturalists' Society. He should have directed the operations, which were somewhat shambolic, but was limited to a watching brief and writing the final report. The work turned into a dig by committee and Ward was hampered by local bigwigs who interfered constantly. His report was considered 'a work of high quality' but the experience scarred him and tended to make him difficult and prickly. He also took an interest in work at Cardiff Castle, proving its Roman origins, and was also involved with investigations at the Roman town of Caerwent. He later penned two monographs on *Romano-British Buildings* and *The Roman Era in Britain,* both published in 1911.

In 1912 Cardiff Museum was absorbed into the National Museum of Wales, and two years later Ward became its first keeper of archaeology. In 1914 he excavated the Tinkinswood long cairn in Glamorgan, one of the earliest scientific digs on this type of site. After the operation he restored the dry-stone walls and strengthened the 40-ton capstone with a brick supporting pillar. Unfortunately, ill-health necessitated his retirement from his post, and he was appointed consulting archaeologist as a mark of the esteem he was held in. He resigned in 1922 and his successor was R. E. M. Wheeler. Ward died the same year, a man of many parts, one of the new breed of scientific archaeologists who worked with precision and communicated the results of his work just as exactly.

# WARNE, Charles (1801–1887).

Charles Warne (1801–87), 'a good and talented Dorset man' was both a barrow-opener and chronicler of the work of other delvers. He was also a keen numismatist.

Described as an individual of 'manly and independent spirit' and 'A good and talented Dorset man' Charles Warne was born in Moreton, Dorset, in July 1801, though the family moved to Pokeswell soon after his birth. After his mother's death in 1838 he settled at Milbourne St Andrew, and moved to London in 1850. Warne's first published piece was on Roman remains found on Kingston Down and issued in 1836, but his real life's work, his research into the Early Bronze Age barrows of Dorset, commenced in 1839 and he did most of his fieldwork between that date and 1862.

The results of his delving into 46 burial mounds were recorded in his *Celtic Tumuli of Dorset*, published in 1866. Warne was also active in the preservation of local monuments, and was instrumental in saving the Maumbury Rings henge near Dorchester from the clutches of the proposed Weymouth Railway. His book contained sections on his own investigations, plus those opened, often imperfectly by his friends (usually the only record of their depredations), and barrows excavated by other activists. The work was typical of its time in its failure to closely locate the tumuli he dug though he did record their composition and structure, and their contents were carefully preserved.

Although many of his barrows took a day or more to open, on one regrettable occasion in September 1848 Warne's party dug into eight mounds on Gussage Down on the same day. He recorded on several occasions the

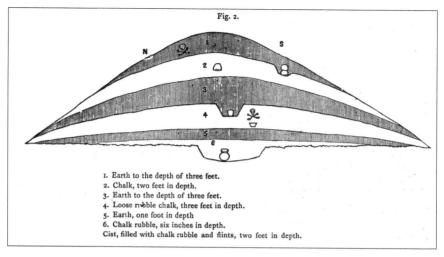

Fig. 2.

1. Earth to the depth of three feet.
2. Chalk, two feet in depth.
3. Earth to the depth of three feet.
4. Loose rubble chalk, three feet in depth.
5. Earth, one foot in depth
6. Chalk rubble, six inches in depth.
Cist, filled with chalk rubble and flints, two feet in depth.

Illustrations are rare in Warne's *Celtic Tumuli of Dorset*, and this basic effort representing a section across a barrow on Lord's Down, Dewlish is a fairly inadequate rarity.

Two fine bucket urns from Warne's collection now form part of his extensive assemblage in Dorset County Museum.

destruction of the downland tumuli for agricultural purposes, noting that one example had been removed 'to promote the fertilization of a crop of turnips.' He also recorded the pointless destruction of some 40 urns found by labourers in a flat cemetery at Rimbury, wantonly smashed by the workmen who set them up as stone-throwing targets when they did not contain the expected treasure! Together with the urns found at Deverel, the Rimbury pots form the Deverel-Rimbury type series.

Warne was elected FSA in 1856, doubtless at the behest of his good friend Charles Roach Smith, with whom he toured the prehistoric and Roman monuments of France in 1853 and 1854. In 1870 he published *Ancient Dorset,* a study of the county from 'Celtic' to Danish times. His 'splendid collection of sepulchral urns and other relics' passed to Dorset County Museum two years before his death. Warne was also an enthusiastic numismatist with a special interest in early coins struck in Dorset. His Roman collection 'was probably unsurpassed' and his personal collection also included a miscellaneous assortment of Roman antiquities excavated at Jordan Hill near Weymouth, presented to him by Thomas Faulkner. His fieldwork also included the research for a map of the county showing all the ancient sites then discovered and published in 1865.

Warne settled in Brighton after some years at Ewell; he died in April 1887 and was buried at Brookwood Cemetery, Woking, 'in a spot chosen by himself, and marked by a massive unhewn obelisk of serpentine stone from Cornwall, also chosen by himself.' 'As long as any account is made of archaeology' wrote his obituarist 'so long will Warne be an honoured name on the lips, in the heart, of the lover of the relics of the olden time.'

# WILLIAMSON, William Crawford (1816–1895).

William Crawford Williamson (1816–95), naturalist and palaeobotanist, is also remembered for his pamphlet on the excavation of the Gristhorpe oak-trunk coffin burial, dug in Yorkshire in 1834.

William Williamson, born in Scarborough in November 1816, was the son of the first curator of the town's Rotunda Museum. Though primarily known as a naturalist and palaeobotanist in which studies he achieved signal fame, it is as a juvenile antiquary that the archaeological world remembers him. He was apprenticed to a Scarborough apothecary, and devoted his spare time to natural history.

As a youthful seventeen-year-old, Williamson attended the opening of a prominent round barrow on Gristhorpe Cliff, south of the Yorkshire resort, in 1834. The tumulus contained a skeleton laid in a lidded and hollowed-out oak-trunk coffin which owed its preservation to the water-holding nature of the boulder clay of which the cliff consisted. The body had been wrapped in animal skins and the bones were stained ebony by the tannic acid in the oak. Gravegoods included a flint tool, two flint arrowheads, a bronze dagger with a bone pommel, a bone pin and a wicker basket. A quantity of vegetable substances were also found inside the coffin, originally described as mistletoe, though these rapidly 'crumbled into dust.'

Until recent times the Gristhorpe burial was exhibited in Scarborough Museum together with his lidded, boat-shaped coffin and accompanying artefacts.

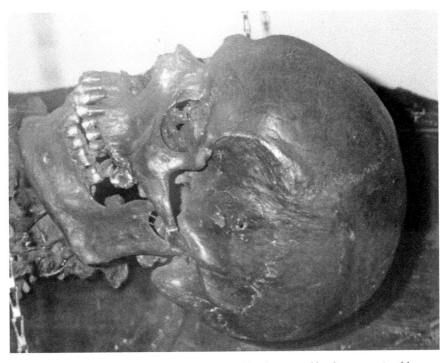

The fine roundheaded skull of the burial was, like the rest of his bones, stained brown through contact with tannic acid in the oak. Sadly, he has now been separated from his coffin and reposes in a glass case.

The rather decayed bones were stabilised, in an early example of conservation, by being boiled in gelatine, this operation being supervised by Williamson himself. They were then rearticulated and returned to the coffin after its removal to Scarborough. Gristhorpe Man is still one of the sights of the museum, though, regrettably to my mind, since the institution has been revamped, he has now been deprived of his coffin. Williamson published a pamphlet entitled *Description of the Tumulus opened at Gristhorpe near Scarborough* (1834) which went through several editions. The dig itself taught an important lesson, not appreciated until that time, that it was possible to construct a picture of early man, in favourable circumstances, by a careful study of the material survivals.

Williamson's later career was based at Manchester, first as a medical practitioner after gaining his MRCS, then from 1851 as professor of natural history at Owens College. He served at the college for over 41 years, retiring in 1892. His work on fossil plants was noteworthy, and gained him his FRS in 1854. Described as spare and erect, with blue-grey eyes set in a round face, he received several honours during his long life, and moved to Clapham after retirement, dying in June 1895. The Gristhorpe dig was his only foray into archaeology, but it was not without its significance for the discipline.

# WITTS, George Backhouse (1846–1912).

George Backhouse Witts (1846–1912), consulting engineer, country gentleman, keen sportsman and antiquary, dug several barrows in Gloucestershire and published an archaeological handbook of his native county.

George Backhouse Witts was born in Upper Slaughter, Gloucestershire in 1846, the son of Edward Francis Witts, the curate of Stanway and grandson of Francis Edward Witts, the noted diarist and rector of Upper Slaughter. The name Backhouse was the maiden name of his paternal grandmother. He was educated at Rugby School and trained as a civil engineer. He was described by his obituarist as having 'an unfailing geniality and bonhomie of manner not only towards his social equals but his social inferiors . . . essentially a Gloucestershire man, in his birth, his upbringing, and in his subsequent career.' His most noted engineering undertaking was the design and supervision of the construction of the Cheltenham to Bourton Railway. Subsequently he acted as consulting engineer to various local drainage and water supply undertakings. A keen sportsman, he was honorary Secretary to the Cotswold Hunt for twenty-six years and served as Conservative agent to the Tewkesbury Division. As a young man he was a lieutenant in the Cheltenham Engineer Volunteers, and also officiated as a JP, a member of the County Council and chairman of his local parish council.

 A keen antiquary, Witts's interest in archaeology seems to have arisen from his fieldwork as a civil engineer, though both his father and grandfather had

Witts is seen here in this view of his home, Hill House, Leckhampton, sitting with his wife and daughters, in the left foreground, nursing the family's pet dog.

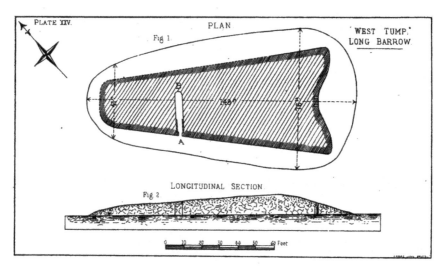

Witts's first operations were carried out in 1880 on the West Tump long barrow which he located by accident whilst out riding. He produced this plan and section of the mound for his later excavation report.

This photograph of the opening shows the only chamber at West Tump which was located on the south-east side of the tumulus. The dry-walling below the pickaxe ran round the side of the mound, whilst the pile at bottom left represents extra-revetment material. Note the collection of human bones visible in front of the spade.

enquiring minds and were interested in antiquities. His father Edward was a noted naturalist who also took a keen interest in geology.

Witts located the West Tump chambered long barrow in 1880, exhuming twenty-three skeletons from the main vault in a dig with George Rolleston. He opened several more long and round barrows in the 1880s, and in 1883 published his *Archaeological Handbook of the County of Gloucester,* wherein he located 40 long barrows, 126 round barrows, 113 hillforts and 'camps' and 26 Roman villas, all delineated on an accompanying map.

Witts was a staunch member of the Bristol and Gloucestershire Archaeological Society, becoming its president in 1896–7. Somewhat of a workaholic, ill-health dogged his later years, and he died in September 1912 at the age of 64.

# Bibliography

| | |
|---|---|
| J. C. Atkinson | *Forty years in a Moorland Parish* (1890) |
| J. Aubrey | *Monumenta Britannica* (1982) |
| T. Bateman | *Vestiges of the Antiquities of Derbyshire* (1848) |
| | *Ten Years' Diggings in Celtic and Saxon Grave-Hills in the Counties of Derby, Stafford and York* (1861) |
| W. C. Borlase | *Naenia Cornubiae* (1872) |
| M. Bowden | *The Life and Work of Lieutenant-General Augustus Henry Lane Fox Pitt Rivers* (2009) |
| W. Boyd Dawkins | *Cave Hunting* (1874) |
| | *Early Man in Britain* (1880) |
| W. Camden | *Britannia* (1586) |
| R. Cunnington | *From Antiquary to Archaeologist* (1975) |
| J. B. Davis | *Crania Britannica* (1865) |
| J. Thurnam | |
| J. Douglas | *Nenia Britannica* (1793) |
| F. Elgee | *Early Man in North-East Yorkshire* (1930) |
| J. Evans | *The Ancient Stone Implements, Weapons and Ornaments of Great Britain and Ireland* (1872) |
| | *The Ancient Bronze Implements, Weapons and Ornaments of Great Britain and Ireland* (1881) |
| B. Faussett | *Inventorum Sepulchrale* (1856) |
| W. Greenwell | *British Barrows* (1877) |
| S. Harrison | *John Robert Mortimer – the life of a 19th century East Yorkshire Archaeologist* (2011) |
| Sir R. C Hoare | *The Ancient history of Wiltshire* ( 2 Vols. 1812, 1821) |
| Revd S. Isaacson | *Barrow-Digging by a Barrow-Knight (1845)* |

| | |
|---|---|
| R. Jessup | *Man of Many Talents – an informal biography of James Douglas* (1975) |
| L. Jewitt | *Grave Mounds and their Contents* (1870) |
| I. Kinnes | *The Greenwell Collection* (1985) |
| I. Longworth | |
| B. M. Marsden | *The Early Barrow Diggers* (3rd Edn. 2011) |
| | *Pioneers of Prehistory* (1984) |
| | *The Barrow Knight – a life of Thomas Bateman, Archaeologist and Collector* (2007) |
| J. Merewether | *Diary of a Dean* (1850) |
| W. A. Miles | *The Deverel Barrow (1826)* |
| J. R. Mortimer | *Forty Years' Researches in British and Saxon Burial Mounds of East Yorkshire* (1905) |
| S. Piggott | *William Stukeley – an Eighteenth-Century Antiquary* (1985) |
| A. H. L. F. Pitt Rivers | *Excavations in Cranborne Chase* (4 vols 1887-98) |
| W. Stukeley | *Stonehenge: A Temple restor'd to the British Druids* (1740) |
| | *Abury: A Temple of the British Druids* (1743) |
| J. Thurnam | *On Ancient British Barrows (Archaeologia 42-43)* (1869–1871) |
| W. M. Turner | *Ancient Remains near Buxton* (1899) |
| C. Warne | *Celtic Tumuli of Dorset* (1866) |
| W. C. Williamson | *Description of the Tumulus opened at Gristhorpe near Scarborough* (1834) |
| G. B. Witts | *Archaeological Handbook of the County of Gloucester* (1883) |
| Revd. C. Woolls | *The Barrow Diggers* (1839) |